THE TRUTH
WILL MAKE
YOU FREE

THE TRUTH WILL MAKE YOU FREE

Compiled by Eugene Carvalho

*To the Body of Christ.
May this compilation bless you richly!
With love…*

TABLE OF CONTENTS

PURPOSE AND ACKNOWLEDGEMENTS

The Infallible, immutable, everlasting, eternal Word of God informs us that the Holy Spirit gives gifts to men and women of the Body of Christ. It states: "the gifts edify the body for the building up of the saints" (Eph. 4:12). I hope the talents and gifts the Lord has given me will be a blessing to someone else through the reading of this compilation.

I am grateful for the love I have received from family members, especially my wife Mercedes. I am also grateful for the knowledge, wisdom and love of many pastors, teachers, and saints that the Lord has used to bless me. Lastly, I must not forget a special thank you to my friend Kathryn Regan for proofreading this material.

THE TRUTH WILL MAKE YOU FREE

The infallible, Word of God for faith, practice and conduct informs us that the Israelites wandered around in the desert for forty years. Moses died and Joshua assumes command of the people of God. God's charge to Joshua is powerful. The Bible says, "This book of the law shall not depart out of thy mouth; but thou shalt meditate therein day and night, that thou mayest observe to do according to all that is written therein: for then thou shalt make thy way prosperous, and then thou shalt have good success"[1] (Jos. 1:8). This was a spiritual solution to help enter the promise land.

The biggest book and the most read book of the Bible is the book of Psalms. The first three verses say, "Blessed is the man that walketh not in the counsel of the ungodly, nor standeth in the way of sinners, nor sitteth in the seat of the scornful. But his delight is in the law of the Lord; and in his law doth he meditate day and night. And he shall be like a tree planted by the rivers of water, that bringeth forth his fruit in his season; his leaf also shall not wither; and whatsoever he doeth shall prosper" (Ps. 1:1-3).

I've preached a three-point message on those three verses many times. The three points are, 1) Be Separated 2) Be Situated 3) Be Saturated. Did you notice point one is to stop keeping company with unbelievers? Because their minds are darkened they will get you to speak death rather than life. Negative speech rather than positive will block your blessings. Individuals are worshipping and serving Jesus or they

---

[1] From this point forward all Scripture quotations, unless otherwise noted, are from the *King James Version.*

are worshipping and serving the devil. There are only two kingdoms: God's and Satan's.

Jesus said the following, "It is the spirit that quickeneth; the flesh profiteth nothing: the words that I speak unto you, they are spirit, and they are life" (Jn. 6:63-70). Jesus' words are spirit. If they are spirit then they are supernatural. The supernatural changes the material and the physical. How do I know? I know the supernatural created the material and the physical. We are informed of that in the first chapter of the Bible.

Words are the most powerful things on earth. They contain life or death. Jesus said His words are spirit and life. The Bible informs us, "Death and life are in the power of the tongue: and they that love it shall eat the fruit thereof" (Pr. 8:21). This is why God informed Joshua, "Do not let the book of the law depart from your mouth" (see Jos. 1:8). If you don't have the word in your heart you will not know what is coming out of your mouth. Individuals are defeated due to what they are speaking. The devil attacks your mind to get you to say the wrong thing regarding your situation or whatever you're having faith for. He has no power. He gets you to use your own power against yourself by deceiving, condemning or tempting you. After he has tricked you the wrong speech comes out of your mouth is what will defeat you. The Bible says. "A good man out of the good treasure of the heart bringeth forth good things: and an evil man out of the evil treasure bringeth forth evil things" (Matt.12:35 KJV). Jesus said, "If ye continue in my word, then are ye my disciples indeed And ye shall know the truth, and the truth shall make you free" (Jn. 8:31-32). With that being said, let's investigate the scriptures that discuss the topic of truth. The truth will make you free.

Chapter Two

TRUTH IN THE OLD TESTAMENT

His Lovingkindness and His Truth

"When the camels had finished drinking, the man took a gold ring weighing a half-shekel and two bracelets for her wrists weighing ten shekels in gold, and said, 'Whose daughter are you? Please tell me, is there room for us to lodge in your father's house?' She said to him, 'I am the daughter of Bethuel, the son of Milcah, whom she bore to Nahor.' Again she said to him, 'We have plenty of both straw and feed, and room to lodge in.' Then the man bowed low and worshiped the Lord. He said, 'Blessed be the Lord, the God of my master Abraham, who has not forsaken His lovingkindness and His truth toward my master; as for me, the Lord has guided me in the way to the house of my master's brothers.' Then the girl ran and told her mother's household about these things"[2] (Ge. 24:22-28).

Whether There Is Truth in You

"But Joseph had recognized his brothers, although they did not recognize him. Joseph remembered the dreams which he had about them, and said to them, 'You are spies; you have come to look at the undefended parts of our land.' Then they said to him, 'No, my lord, but your servants have come to buy food. We are all sons of one man; we are honest men, your servants are not spies.' Yet he said to them, 'No, but you have come to look at the undefended parts of our land!' But they said, 'Your servants are twelve

---

[2] From this point forward all Scripture quotations, unless otherwise noted, are from the *New American Standard Bible*.

brothers in all, the sons of one man in the land of Canaan; and behold, the youngest is with our father today, and one is no longer alive.' Joseph said to them, 'It is as I said to you, you are spies; by this you will be tested: by the life of Pharaoh, you shall not go from this place unless your youngest brother comes here! Send one of you that he may get your brother, while you remain confined, that your words may be tested, whether there is truth in you. But if not, by the life of Pharaoh, surely you are spies.' So he put them all together in prison for three days" (Ge. 42:8-17).

Men of Truth, Those Who Hate Dishonest Gain

"It came about the next day that Moses sat to judge the people, and the people stood about Moses from the morning until the evening. Now when Moses' father-in-law saw all that he was doing for the people, he said, 'What is this thing that you are doing for the people? Why do you alone sit as judge and all the people stand about you from morning until evening?' Moses said to his father-in-law, 'Because the people come to me to inquire of God. When they have a dispute, it comes to me, and I judge between a man and his neighbor and make known the statutes of God and His laws.' Moses' father-in-law said to him, 'The thing that you are doing is not good. You will surely wear out, both yourself and these people who are with you, for the task is too heavy for you; you cannot do it alone. Now listen to me: I will give you counsel, and God be with you. You be the people's representative before God, and you bring the disputes to God, then teach them the statutes and the laws, and make known to them the way in which they are to walk and the work they are to do. Furthermore, you shall select out of all the people able men who fear God, men of truth, those who hate dishonest gain; and you shall place these over them as leaders of thousands, of hundreds, of fifties and of tens. Let them judge the people at all times; and let it be that every major dispute they will bring to you, but every minor dispute they themselves will judge. So it will be easier for you, and they will bear the burden with you. If you do this thing and God so commands you, then you will be able to endure, and all these people also will go to their place in peace'" (Ex. 18:13-23).

Abounding in Lovingkindness and Truth

"Now the Lord said to Moses, 'Cut out for yourself two stone tablets like the former ones, and I will write on the tablets the words that were on the former tablets which you shattered. So be ready by morning, and come up in the morning to Mount Sinai, and present yourself there to Me on the top of the mountain. No man is to come up with you, nor let any man be seen anywhere on the mountain; even the flocks and the herds may not graze in front of that mountain.' So he cut out two stone tablets like the former ones, and Moses rose up early in the morning and went up to Mount Sinai, as the Lord had commanded him, and he took two stone tablets in his hand. The Lord descended in the cloud and stood there with him as he called upon the name of the Lord. Then the Lord passed by in front of him and proclaimed, 'The Lord, the Lord God, compassionate and gracious, slow to anger, and abounding in lovingkindness and truth; who keeps lovingkindness for thousands, who forgives iniquity, transgression and sin; yet He will by no means leave the guilty unpunished, visiting the iniquity of fathers on the children and on the grandchildren to the third and fourth generations.' Moses made haste to bow low toward the earth and worship. He said, 'If now I have found favor in Your sight, O Lord, I pray, let the Lord go along in our midst, even though the people are so obstinate, and pardon our iniquity and our sin, and take us as Your own possession'" (Ex. 34:1-9).

Give Me a Pledge of Truth

"Now before they lay down, she came up to them on the roof, and said to the men, 'I know that the Lord has given you the land, and that the terror of you has fallen on us, and that all the inhabitants of the land have melted away before you. For we have heard how the Lord dried up the water of the Red Sea before you when you came out of Egypt, and what you did to the two kings of the Amorites who were beyond the Jordan, to Sihon and Og, whom you utterly destroyed. When we heard it, our hearts melted and no courage remained in any man any longer because of you; for the Lord your God, He is God in heaven above and on earth beneath. Now therefore, please swear to me by the Lord, since I have dealt kindly with you, that you also will deal kindly with my father's household, and give me a pledge of truth, and spare my father and my mother and my brothers and my sisters, with all who belong to them, and deliver our lives from death.' So the men said to her, 'Our life for yours if you do not tell this business of ours; and it shall come about when the Lord gives us the land that we will deal kindly and faithfully with you'" (Jos. 2:8-14).

Chapter Two

Serve Him in Sincerity and Truth

"Now, therefore, fear the Lord and serve Him in sincerity and truth; and put away the gods which your fathers served beyond the River and in Egypt, and serve the Lord. If it is disagreeable in your sight to serve the Lord, choose for yourselves today whom you will serve: whether the gods which your fathers served which were beyond the River, or the gods of the Amorites in whose land you are living; but as for me and my house, we will serve the Lord" (Jos 24:14-15).

In Truth You Are Anointing Me

"Now when they told Jotham, he went and stood on the top of Mount Gerizim, and lifted his voice and called out. Thus he said to them, 'Listen to me, O men of Shechem, that God may listen to you. Once the trees went forth to anoint a king over them, and they said to the olive tree, "Reign over us!" But the olive tree said to them, "Shall I leave my fatness with which God and men are honored, and go to wave over the trees?" Then the trees said to the fig tree, "You come, reign over us!" But the fig tree said to them, "Shall I leave my sweetness and my good fruit, and go to wave over the trees?" Then the trees said to the vine, "You come, reign over us!" But the vine said to them, "Shall I leave my new wine, which cheers God and men, and go to wave over the trees?' Finally all the trees said to the bramble, "You come, reign over us!" The bramble said to the trees, "If in truth you are anointing me as king over you, come and take refuge in my shade; but if not, may fire come out from the bramble and consume the cedars of Lebanon"'" (Jdg. 9:7-15).

If You Have Dealt in Truth and Integrity

"Now therefore, if you have dealt in truth and integrity in making Abimelech king, and if you have dealt well with Jerubbaal and his house, and have dealt with him as he deserved — for my father fought for you and risked his life and delivered you from the hand of Midian; but you have risen against my father's house today and have killed his sons, seventy men, on one stone, and have made Abimelech, the son of his maidservant, king over the men of Shechem, because he is your relative — if then you have dealt in truth and integrity with Jerubbaal and his house this day, rejoice in Abimelech, and let him also rejoice in you. But if not, let fire come out from Abimelech and consume the men of Shechem and Beth-millo; and let fire come out from the men of Shechem and from Beth-millo, and consume Abimelech. Then Jotham escaped and fled, and went to Beer and remained there because of Abimelech his brother" (Jdg. 9:16-21).

Serve Him in Truth with All Your Heart

"Then all the people said to Samuel, 'Pray for your servants to the Lord your God, so that we may not die, for we have added to all our sins this evil by asking for ourselves a king.' Samuel said to the people, 'Do not fear. You have committed all this evil, yet do not turn aside from following the Lord, but serve the Lord with all your heart. You must not turn aside, for then you would go after futile things which can not profit or deliver, because they are futile. For the Lord will not abandon His people on account of His great name, because the Lord has been pleased to make you a people for Himself. Moreover, as for me, far be it from me that I should sin against the Lord by ceasing to pray for you; but I will instruct you in the good and right way. Only fear the Lord and serve Him in truth with all your heart; for consider what great things He has done for you. But if you still do wickedly, both you and your king will be swept away'" (1Sa. 12:19-25).

Show Lovingkindness and Truth to You

"Then it came about afterwards that David inquired of the Lord, saying, 'Shall I go up to one of the cities of Judah?' And the Lord said to him, 'Go up.' So David said, 'Where shall I go up?' And He said, 'To Hebron.' So David went up there, and his two wives also, Ahinoam the Jezreelitess and Abigail the widow of Nabal the Carmelite. And David brought up his men who were with him, each with his household; and they lived in the cities of Hebron. Then the men of Judah came and there anointed David king over the house of Judah. And they told David, saying, 'It was the men of Jabesh-gilead who buried Saul.' David sent messengers to the men of Jabesh-gilead, and said to them, 'May you be blessed of the Lord because you have shown this kindness to Saul your lord, and have buried him. Now may the Lord show lovingkindness and truth to you; and I also will show this goodness to you, because you have done this thing. Now therefore, let your hands be strong and be valiant; for Saul your lord is dead, and also the house of Judah has anointed me king over them'" (2Sa. 2:1-7).

You are God, and Your Words are Truth

"Then David the king went in and sat before the Lord, and he said, 'Who am I, O Lord God, and what is my house, that You have brought me this far? And yet this was insignificant in Your eyes, O Lord God, for You have spoken also of the house of Your servant concerning the distant future. And this is the custom of man, O Lord God. Again what more can David say to You? For You know Your servant, O Lord God! For the sake of Your word, and according to Your own heart, You have done all this greatness to let Your servant know. For this reason You are great, O Lord God; for there is none like You, and there is no God besides You, according to all that we have heard with our ears. And what one nation on the earth is like Your people Israel, whom God went to redeem for Himself as a people and to make a name for Himself, and to do a great thing for You and awesome things for Your land, before Your people whom You have redeemed for Yourself from Egypt, from nations and their gods? For You have established for Yourself Your people Israel as Your own people forever, and You, O Lord, have become their God. Now therefore, O Lord God, the word that You have spoken concerning Your servant and his house, confirm it forever, and do as You have spoken, that Your name may be magnified forever, by saying, "The Lord of hosts is God over Israel"; and may the house of Your servant David be established before You. For You, O Lord of hosts, the God of Israel, have made a revelation to Your servant, saying, "I will build you a house"; therefore Your servant has found courage to pray this prayer to You. Now, O Lord God, You are God, and Your words are truth, and You have promised this good thing to Your servant. Now therefore, may it please You to bless the house of Your servant, that it may continue forever before You. For You, O Lord God, have spoken; and with Your blessing may the house of Your servant be blessed forever'" (2Sa. 7:18-29).

Mercy and Truth Be with You

"Then the king said to Ittai the Gittite, 'Why will you also go with us? Return and remain with the king, for you are a foreigner and also an exile; return to your own place. You came only yesterday, and shall I today make you wander with us, while I go where I will? Return and take back your brothers; mercy and truth be with you.' But Ittai answered the king and said, 'As the Lord lives, and as my lord the king lives, surely wherever my lord the king may be, whether for death or for life, there also your servant will be." Therefore David said to Ittai, 'Go and pass over.' So Ittai the Gittite passed over with all his men and all the little ones who were with him. While all the country was weeping with a loud voice, all the people passed over. The king also passed over the brook Kidron, and all the people passed over toward the way of the wilderness" (2Sa. 15:19-23).

In Truth with All Their Heart

"As David's time to die drew near, he charged Solomon his son, saying, 'I am going the way of all the earth. Be strong, therefore, and show yourself a man. Keep the charge of the Lord your God, to walk in His ways, to keep His statutes, His commandments, His ordinances, and His testimonies, according to what is written in the Law of Moses, that you may succeed in all that you do and wherever you turn, so that the Lord may carry out His promise which He spoke concerning me, saying, "If your sons are careful of their way, to walk before Me in truth with all their heart and with all their soul, you shall not lack a man on the throne of Israel"'" (1Ki. 2:1-4).

In Truth, Righteousness and Uprightness of Heart

"Now Solomon loved the Lord, walking in the statutes of his father David, except he sacrificed and burned incense on the high places. The king went to Gibeon to sacrifice there, for that was the great high place; Solomon offered a thousand burnt offerings on that altar. In Gibeon the Lord appeared to Solomon in a dream at night; and God said, 'Ask what you wish me to give you.' Then Solomon said, "You have shown great lovingkindness to Your servant David my father, according as he walked before You in truth and righteousness and uprightness of heart toward You; and You have reserved for him this great lovingkindness, that You have given him a son to sit on his throne, as it is this day. Now, O Lord my God, You have made Your servant king in place of my father David, yet I am but a little child; I do not know how to go out or come in. Your servant is in the midst of Your people which You have chosen, a great people who are too many to be numbered or counted. So give Your servant an understanding heart to judge Your people to discern between good and evil. For who is able to judge this great people of Yours" (1Ki. 3:3-9)?

That the Word of the Lord in Your Mouth Is Truth

"Now it came about after these things that the son of the woman, the mistress of the house, became sick; and his sickness was so severe that there was no breath left in him. So she said to Elijah, 'What do I have to do with you, O man of God? You have come to me to bring my iniquity to remembrance and to put my son to death!" He said to her, 'Give me your son.' Then he took him from her bosom and carried him up to the upper room where he was living, and laid him on his own bed. He called to the Lord and said, 'O Lord my God, have You also brought calamity to the widow with whom I am staying, by causing her son to die?' Then he stretched himself upon the child three times, and called to the Lord and said, 'O Lord my God, I pray You, let this child's life return to him.' The Lord heard the voice of Elijah, and the life of the child returned to him and he revived. Elijah took the child and brought him down from the upper room into the house and gave him to his mother; and Elijah said, 'See, your son is alive.' Then the woman said to Elijah, 'Now I know that you are a man of God and that the word of the Lord in your mouth is truth'" (1Ki. 17:17-24).

I Adjure You to Speak to Me Nothing but the Truth

"When he came to the king, the king said to him, 'Micaiah, shall we go to Ramoth-gilead to battle, or shall we refrain?' And he answered him, 'Go up and succeed, and the Lord will give it into the hand of the king.' Then the king said to him, 'How many times must I adjure you to speak to me nothing but the truth in the name of the Lord?' So he said, 'I saw all Israel Scattered on the mountains, Like sheep which have no shepherd.' And the Lord said, 'These have no master. Let each of them return to his house in peace'" (1Ki. 22:15-17).

Chapter Two

In Truth and with a Whole Heart

"In those days Hezekiah became mortally ill. And Isaiah the prophet the son of Amoz came to him and said to him, 'Thus says the Lord, "Set your house in order, for you shall die and not live."' Then he turned his face to the wall and prayed to the Lord, saying, 'Remember now, O Lord, I beseech You, how I have walked before You in truth and with a whole heart and have done what is good in Your sight.' And Hezekiah wept bitterly. Before Isaiah had gone out of the middle court, the word of the Lord came to him, saying, 'Return and say to Hezekiah the leader of My people, "Thus says the Lord, the God of your father David, 'I have heard your prayer, I have seen your tears; behold, I will heal you. On the third day you shall go up to the house of the Lord. I will add fifteen years to your life, and I will deliver you and this city from the hand of the king of Assyria; and I will defend this city for My own sake and for My servant David's sake.'"' Then Isaiah said, 'Take a cake of figs.' And they took and laid it on the boil, and he recovered" (2Ki. 20:1-7).

If There Will Be Peace and Truth in My Days

"Then Isaiah said to Hezekiah, "Hear the word of the Lord. "Behold, the days are coming when all that is in your house, and all that your fathers have laid up in store to this day will be carried to Babylon; nothing shall be left," says the Lord. "Some of your sons who shall issue from you, whom you will beget, will be taken away; and they will become officials in the palace of the king of Babylon.'" Then Hezekiah said to Isaiah, 'The word of the Lord which you have spoken is good.' For he thought, 'Is it not so, if there will be peace and truth in my days'" (2Ki. 20:16-19)?

Speak to Me Nothing but the Truth

"When he came to the king, the king said to him, 'Micaiah, shall we go to Ramoth-gilead to battle, or shall I refrain?' He said, 'Go up and succeed, for they will be given into your hand.' Then the king said to him, 'How many times must I adjure you to speak to me nothing but the truth in the name of the Lord?' So he said, 'I saw all Israel Scattered on the mountains, Like sheep which have no shepherd; And the Lord said, "These have no master. Let each of them return to his house in peace."' Then the king of Israel said to Jehoshaphat, 'Did I not tell you that he would not prophesy good concerning me, but evil'" (2Ch. 18:14-17)?

Namely, Words of Peace and Truth

"Then Queen Esther, daughter of Abihail, with Mordecai the Jew, wrote with full authority to confirm this second letter about Purim. He sent letters to all the Jews, to the 127 provinces of the kingdom of Ahasuerus, namely, words of peace and truth, to establish these days of Purim at their appointed times, just as Mordecai the Jew and Queen Esther had established for them, and just as they had established for themselves and for their descendants with instructions for their times of fasting and their lamentations. The command of Esther established these customs for Purim, and it was written in the book" (Est. 9:29-32).

Chapter Two

In Truth I Know that This Is So

"Then Job answered, 'In truth I know that this is so; But how can a man be in the right before God? If one wished to dispute with Him, He could not answer Him once in a thousand times. Wise in heart and mighty in strength, Who has defied Him without harm? It is God who removes the mountains, they know not how, When He overturns them in His anger; Who shakes the earth out of its place, And its pillars tremble; Who commands the sun not to shine, And sets a seal upon the stars; Who alone stretches out the heavens And tramples down the waves of the sea; Who makes the Bear, Orion and the Pleiades, And the chambers of the south; Who does great things, unfathomable, And wondrous works without number. Were He to pass by me, I would not see Him; Were He to move past me, I would not perceive Him. Were He to snatch away, who could restrain Him? Who could say to Him, "What are You doing"'" (Job 9:1-12)?

Speaks Truth in His Heart

"O Lord, who may abide in Your tent? Who may dwell on Your holy hill? He who walks with integrity, and works righteousness, And speaks truth in his heart. He does not slander with his tongue, Nor does evil to his neighbor, Nor takes up a reproach against his friend; In whose eyes a reprobate is despised, But who honors those who fear the Lord; He swears to his own hurt and does not change; He does not put out his money at interest, Nor does he take a bribe against the innocent. He who does these things will never be shaken" (Ps. 15:1-5).

Chapter Two

Lead Me in Your Truth and Teach Me

"Make me know Your ways, O Lord; Teach me Your paths. Lead me in Your truth and teach me, For You are the God of my salvation; For You I wait all the day. Remember, O Lord, Your compassion and Your lovingkindnesses, For they have been from of old. Do not remember the sins of my youth or my transgressions; According to Your lovingkindness remember me, For Your goodness' sake, O Lord" (Ps. 25:4-7).

The Paths of the Lord are Lovingkindness and Truth

"Good and upright is the Lord; Therefore He instructs sinners in the way. He leads the humble in justice, And He teaches the humble His way. All the paths of the Lord are lovingkindness and truth To those who keep His covenant and His testimonies. For Your name's sake, O Lord, Pardon my iniquity, for it is great" (Ps. 25:8-11).

I Have Walked in Your Truth

"Vindicate me, O Lord, for I have walked in my integrity, And I have trusted in the Lord without wavering. Examine me, O Lord, and try me; Test my mind and my heart. For Your lovingkindness is before my eyes, And I have walked in Your truth. I do not sit with deceitful men, Nor will I go with pretenders. I hate the assembly of evildoers, And I will not sit with the wicked. I shall wash my hands in innocence, And I will go about Your altar, O Lord, That I may proclaim with the voice of thanksgiving And declare all Your wonders" (Ps. 26:1-7).

Chapter Two

You Have Ransomed Me, O Lord, God of Truth

"In You, O Lord, I have taken refuge; Let me never be ashamed; In Your righteousness deliver me. Incline Your ear to me, rescue me quickly; Be to me a rock of strength, A stronghold to save me. For You are my rock and my fortress; For Your name's sake You will lead me and guide me. You will pull me out of the net which they have secretly laid for me, For You are my strength. Into Your hand I commit my spirit; You have ransomed me, O Lord, God of truth" (Ps. 31:1-5).

Your Truth from the Great Congregation

"I have proclaimed glad tidings of righteousness in the great congregation; Behold, I will not restrain my lips, O Lord, You know. I have not hidden Your righteousness within my heart; I have spoken of Your faithfulness and Your salvation; I have not concealed Your lovingkindness and Your truth from the great congregation" (Ps. 40:9-10).

Your Truth Will Continually Preserve Me

"You, O Lord, will not withhold Your compassion from me; Your lovingkindness and Your truth will continually preserve me. For evils beyond number have surrounded me; My iniquities have overtaken me, so that I am not able to see; They are more numerous than the hairs of my head, And my heart has failed me" (Ps. 40:11-12).

O Send Out Your Light and Your Truth

"O send out Your light and Your truth, let them lead me; Let them bring me to Your holy hill And to Your dwelling places. Then I will go to the altar of God, To God my exceeding joy; And upon the lyre I shall praise You, O God, my God" (Ps. 43:3-4).

For the Cause of Truth and Meekness

"Gird Your sword on Your thigh, O Mighty One, In Your splendor and Your majesty! And in Your majesty ride on victoriously, For the cause of truth and meekness and righteousness; Let Your right hand teach You awesome things. Your arrows are sharp; The peoples fall under You; Your arrows are in the heart of the King's enemies. Your throne, O God, is forever and ever; A scepter of uprightness is the scepter of Your kingdom. You have loved righteousness and hated wickedness; Therefore God, Your God, has anointed You With the oil of joy above Your fellows. All Your garments are fragrant with myrrh and aloes and cassia; Out of ivory palaces stringed instruments have made You glad. Kings' daughters are among Your noble ladies; At Your right hand stands the queen in gold from Ophir" (Ps. 45:3-9).

Behold, You Desire Truth in the Innermost Being

"Behold, I was brought forth in iniquity, And in sin my mother conceived me. Behold, You desire truth in the innermost being, And in the hidden part You will make me know wisdom. Purify me with hyssop, and I shall be clean; Wash me, and I shall be whiter than snow. Make me to hear joy and gladness, Let the bones which You have broken rejoice. Hide Your face from my sins And blot out all my iniquities" (Ps. 51:5-9).

Send Forth His Lovingkindness and His Truth

"Be gracious to me, O God, be gracious to me, For my soul takes refuge in You; And in the shadow of Your wings I will take refuge Until destruction passes by. I will cry to God Most High, To God who accomplishes all things for me. He will send from heaven and save me; He reproaches him who tramples upon me. Selah. God will send forth His lovingkindness and His truth" (Ps. 57:1-3).

Your Truth to the Clouds

"My heart is steadfast, O God, my heart is steadfast; I will sing, yes, I will sing praises! Awake, my glory! Awake, harp and lyre! I will awaken the dawn. I will give thanks to You, O Lord, among the peoples; I will sing praises to You among the nations. For Your lovingkindness is great to the heavens And Your truth to the clouds. Be exalted above the heavens, O God; Let Your glory be above all the earth" (Ps. 57:7-11).

It May Be Displayed Because of the Truth

"O God, You have rejected us. You have broken us; You have been angry; O, restore us. You have made the land quake, You have split it open; Heal its breaches, for it totters. You have made Your people experience hardship; You have given us wine to drink that makes us stagger. You have given a banner to those who fear You, That it may be displayed because of the truth. That Your beloved may be delivered, Save with Your right hand, and answer us" (Ps. 60:1-5)!

Appoint Lovingkindness and Truth

"For You have heard my vows, O God; You have given me the inheritance of those who fear Your name. You will prolong the king's life; His years will be as many generations. He will abide before God forever; Appoint lovingkindness and truth that they may preserve him. So I will sing praise to Your name forever, That I may pay my vows day by day" (Ps. 61:5-8).

Answer Me with Your Saving Truth

"But as for me, my prayer is to You, O Lord, at an acceptable time; O God, in the greatness of Your lovingkindness, Answer me with Your saving truth. Deliver me from the mire and do not let me sink; May I be delivered from my foes and from the deep waters. May the flood of water not overflow me Nor the deep swallow me up, Nor the pit shut its mouth on me" (Ps. 69:13-15).

Even Your Truth, O My God

"I will also praise You with a harp, Even Your truth, O my God; To You I will sing praises with the lyre, O Holy One of Israel. My lips will shout for joy when I sing praises to You; And my soul, which You have redeemed. My tongue also will utter Your righteousness all day long; For they are ashamed, for they are humiliated who seek my hurt" (Ps. 71:22-24).

Lovingkindness and Truth Have Met Together

"I will hear what God the Lord will say; For He will speak peace to His people, to His godly ones; But let them not turn back to folly. Surely His salvation is near to those who fear Him, That glory may dwell in our land. Lovingkindness and truth have met together; Righteousness and peace have kissed each other. Truth springs from the earth, And righteousness looks down from heaven. Indeed, the Lord will give what is good, And our land will yield its produce. Righteousness will go before Him And will make His footsteps into a way" (Ps. 85:8-13).

O Lord; I Will Walk in Your Truth

"Teach me Your way, O Lord; I will walk in Your truth; Unite my heart to fear Your name. I will give thanks to You, O Lord my God, with all my heart, And will glorify Your name forever. For Your lovingkindness toward me is great, And You have delivered my soul from the depths of Sheol" (Ps. 86:11-13).

Abundant in Lovingkindness and Truth

"O God, arrogant men have risen up against me, And a band of violent men have sought my life, And they have not set You before them. But You, O Lord, are a God merciful and gracious, Slow to anger and abundant in lovingkindness and truth. Turn to me, and be gracious to me; Oh grant Your strength to Your servant, And save the son of Your handmaid. Show me a sign for good, That those who hate me may see it and be ashamed, Because You, O Lord, have helped me and comforted me" (Ps. 86:14-17).

Lovingkindness and Truth Go Before You

"The heavens are Yours, the earth also is Yours; The world and all it contains, You have founded them. The north and the south, You have created them; Tabor and Hermon shout for joy at Your name. You have a strong arm; Your hand is mighty, Your right hand is exalted. Righteousness and justice are the foundation of Your throne; Lovingkindness and truth go before You. How blessed are the people who know the joyful sound! O Lord, they walk in the light of Your countenance. In Your name they rejoice all the day, And by Your righteousness they are exalted. For You are the glory of their strength, And by Your favor our horn is exalted. For our shield belongs to the Lord, And our king to the Holy One of Israel" (Ps. 89:11-18).

Your Truth Reaches to the Skies

"My heart is steadfast, O God; I will sing, I will sing praises, even with my soul. Awake, harp and lyre; I will awaken the dawn! I will give thanks to You, O Lord, among the peoples, And I will sing praises to You among the nations. For Your lovingkindness is great above the heavens, And Your truth reaches to the skies. Be exalted, O God, above the heavens, And Your glory above all the earth. That Your beloved may be delivered, Save with Your right hand, and answer me" (Ps. 108:1-6)!`

Chapter Two

The Works of His Hands Are Truth and Justice

"The works of His hands are truth and justice; All His precepts are sure. They are upheld forever and ever; They are performed in truth and uprightness. He has sent redemption to His people; He has ordained His covenant forever; Holy and awesome is His name. The fear of the Lord is the beginning of wisdom; A good understanding have all those who do His commandments; His praise endures forever" (Ps. 111:7-10).

Because of Your Truth

"Not to us, O Lord, not to us, But to Your name give glory Because of Your lovingkindness, because of Your truth. Why should the nations say, 'Where, now, is their God?' But our God is in the heavens; He does whatever He pleases. Their idols are silver and gold, The work of man's hands. They have mouths, but they cannot speak; They have eyes, but they cannot see; They have ears, but they cannot hear; They have noses, but they cannot smell; They have hands, but they cannot feel; They have feet, but they cannot walk; They cannot make a sound with their throat. Those who make them will become like them, Everyone who trusts in them" (Ps. 115:1-8).

The Truth of the Lord Is Everlasting

"Praise the Lord, all nations; Laud Him, all peoples! For His lovingkindness is great toward us, And the truth of the Lord is everlasting. Praise the Lord" (Ps. 117:1-2)!

Do Not Take the Word of Truth Out of My Mouth

"May Your lovingkindnesses also come to me, O Lord, Your salvation according to Your word; So I will have an answer for him who reproaches me, For I trust in Your word. And do not take the word of truth utterly out of my mouth, For I wait for Your ordinances. So I will keep Your law continually, Forever and ever. And I will walk at liberty, For I seek Your precepts. I will also speak of Your testimonies before kings And shall not be ashamed. I shall delight in Your commandments, Which I love. And I shall lift up my hands to Your commandments, Which I love; And I will meditate on Your statutes" (Ps. 119:41-48).

Your Law Is Truth

"Righteous are You, O Lord, And upright are Your judgments. You have commanded Your testimonies in righteousness And exceeding faithfulness. My zeal has consumed me, Because my adversaries have forgotten Your words. Your word is very pure, Therefore Your servant loves it. I am small and despised, Yet I do not forget Your precepts. Your righteousness is an everlasting righteousness, And Your law is truth. Trouble and anguish have come upon me, Yet Your commandments are my delight. Your testimonies are righteous forever; Give me understanding that I may live" (Ps. 119:137-144).

All Your Commandments Are Truth

"I cried with all my heart; answer me, O Lord! I will observe Your statutes. I cried to You; save me And I shall keep Your testimonies. I rise before dawn and cry for help; I wait for Your words. My eyes anticipate the night watches, That I may meditate on Your word. Hear my voice according to Your lovingkindness; Revive me, O Lord, according to Your ordinances. Those who follow after wickedness draw near; They are far from Your law. You are near, O Lord, And all Your commandments are truth. Of old I have known from Your testimonies That You have founded them forever" (Ps. 119:145-152).

The Sum of Your Word Is Truth

"Look upon my affliction and rescue me, For I do not forget Your law. Plead my cause and redeem me; Revive me according to Your word. Salvation is far from the wicked, For they do not seek Your statutes. Great are Your mercies, O Lord; Revive me according to Your ordinances. Many are my persecutors and my adversaries, Yet I do not turn aside from Your testimonies. I behold the treacherous and loathe them, Because they do not keep Your word. Consider how I love Your precepts; Revive me, O Lord, according to Your lovingkindness. The sum of Your word is truth, And every one of Your righteous ordinances is everlasting" (Ps. 119:153-160).

A Truth from Which He Will Not Turn Back

"For the sake of David Your servant, Do not turn away the face of Your anointed. The Lord has sworn to David A truth from which He will not turn back: Of the fruit of your body I will set upon your throne. If your sons will keep My covenant And My testimony which I will teach them, Their sons also shall sit upon your throne forever" (Ps. 132:10-12).

Your Lovingkindness and Your Truth

"I will give You thanks with all my heart; I will sing praises to You before the gods. I will bow down toward Your holy temple And give thanks to Your name for Your lovingkindness and Your truth; For You have magnified Your word according to all Your name. On the day I called, You answered me; You made me bold with strength in my soul" (Ps. 138:1-3).

To All Who Call Upon Him in Truth

"The Lord is righteous in all His ways And kind in all His deeds. The Lord is near to all who call upon Him, To all who call upon Him in truth. He will fulfill the desire of those who fear Him; He will also hear their cry and will save them. The Lord keeps all who love Him, But all the wicked He will destroy. My mouth will speak the praise of the Lord, And all flesh will bless His holy name forever and ever" (Ps. 145:17-21).

Do Not Let Kindness and Truth Leave You

"Do not let kindness and truth leave you; Bind them around your neck, Write them on the tablet of your heart" (Pr. 3:3).

For My Mouth Will Utter Truth

"For my mouth will utter truth; And wickedness is an abomination to my lips" (Pr. 8:7).

He Who Speaks Truth Tells What Is Right

"He who speaks truth tells what is right, But a false witness, deceit" (Pr. 12:17).

Truth Will Be to Those Who Devise Good

"Will they not go astray who devise evil? But kindness and truth will be to those who devise good" (Pr. 14:22).

By Lovingkindness and Truth Iniquity Is Atoned

"By lovingkindness and truth iniquity is atoned for, And by the fear of the Lord one keeps away from evil" (Pr. 16:6).

Loyalty and Truth Preserve the King

"Loyalty and truth preserve the king, And he upholds his throne by righteousness" (Pr. 20:28).

The Man Who Listens to the Truth Speaks Forever

"A false witness will perish, But the man who listens to the truth will speak forever" (Pr. 21:28).

You Know the Certainty of the Words of Truth

"To make you know the certainty of the words of truth That you may correctly answer him who sent you" (Pr. 22:21)?

Buy Truth, and Do Not Sell It

"Buy truth, and do not sell it, Get wisdom and instruction and understanding" (Pr. 23:23).

If a King Judges the Poor with Truth

"If a king judges the poor with truth, His throne will be established forever" (Pr. 29:14).

Write Words of Truth Correctly

"In addition to being a wise man, the Preacher also taught the people knowledge; and he pondered, searched out and arranged many proverbs. The Preacher sought to find delightful words and to write words of truth correctly" (Ecc. 12:9-10).

Those Who Err in Mind Will Know the Truth

"Therefore thus says the Lord, who redeemed Abraham, concerning the house of Jacob: "Jacob shall not now be ashamed, nor shall his face now turn pale; But when he sees his children, the work of My hands, in his midst, They will sanctify My name; Indeed, they will sanctify the Holy One of Jacob And will stand in awe of the God of Israel. Those who err in mind will know the truth, And those who criticize will accept instruction'" (Is. 29:22-24).

The Mind of the Hasty Will Discern the Truth

"Behold, a king will reign righteously And princes will rule justly. Each will be like a refuge from the wind And a shelter from the storm, Like streams of water in a dry country, Like the shade of a huge rock in a parched land. Then the eyes of those who see will not be blinded, And the ears of those who hear will listen. The mind of the hasty will discern the truth, And the tongue of the stammerers will hasten to speak clearly. No longer will the fool be called noble, Or the rogue be spoken of as generous. For a fool speaks nonsense, And his heart inclines toward wickedness: To practice ungodliness and to speak error against the Lord, To keep the hungry person unsatisfied And to withhold drink from the thirsty. As for a rogue, his weapons are evil; He devises wicked schemes To destroy the afflicted with slander, Even though the needy one speaks what is right. But the noble man devises noble plans; And by noble plans he stands" (Is. 32:1-8).

How I Have Walked Before You in Truth

"In those days Hezekiah became mortally ill. And Isaiah the prophet the son of Amoz came to him and said to him, 'Thus says the Lord, "Set your house in order, for you hall die and not live."' Then Hezekiah turned his face to the wall and prayed to the Lord, and said, "Remember now, O Lord, I beseech You, how I have walked before You in truth and with a whole heart, and have done what is good in Your sight.' And Hezekiah wept bitterly" (Is.. 38:1-3).

There Will Be Peace and Truth

"Then Isaiah said to Hezekiah, 'Hear the word of the Lord of hosts, '"Behold, the days are coming when all that is in your house and all that your fathers have laid up in store to this day will be carried to Babylon; nothing will be left," says the Lord. "And some of your sons who will issue from you, whom you will beget, will be taken away, and they will become officials in the palace of the king of Babylon.'" Then Hezekiah said to Isaiah, 'The word of the Lord which you have spoken is good.' For he thought, 'For there will be peace and truth in my days'" (Is. 39:5-8).

Will Be Blessed by the God of Truth

"Therefore, thus says the Lord God, "Behold, My servants will eat, but you will be hungry. Behold, My servants will drink, but you will be thirsty. Behold, My servants will rejoice, but you will be put to shame. Behold, My servants will shout joyfully with a glad heart, But you will cry out with a heavy heart, And you will wail with a broken spirit. You will leave your name for a curse to My chosen ones, And the Lord God will slay you. But My servants will be called by another name. Because he who is blessed in the earth Will be blessed by the God of truth; And he who swears in the earth Will swear by the God of truth; Because the former troubles are forgotten, And because they are hidden from My sight'" (Is. 65:13-16)!

In Truth, in Justice and in Righteousness

"'If you will return, O Israel," declares the Lord, 'Then you should return to Me. And if you will put away your detested things from My presence, And will not waver, And you will swear, 'As the Lord lives,' In truth, in justice and in righteousness; Then the nations will bless themselves in Him, And in Him they will glory.' For thus says the Lord to the men of Judah and to Jerusalem, 'Break up your fallow ground, And do not sow among thorns'" (Jer. 4:1-3).

Chapter Two

Who Does Justice, Who Seeks Truth

'Roam to and fro through the streets of Jerusalem, And look now and take note. And seek in her open squares, If you can find a man, If there is one who does justice, who seeks truth, Then I will pardon her. And although they say, "As the Lord lives," Surely they swear falsely.' O Lord, do not Your eyes look for truth? You have smitten them, But they did not weaken; You have consumed them, But they refused to take correction. They have made their faces harder than rock; They have refused to repent" (Jer. 5:1-3).

Truth Has Perished and Has Been Cut Off

'You shall speak all these words to them, but they will not listen to you; and you shall call to them, but they will not answer you. You shall say to them, "This is the nation that did not obey the voice of the Lord their God or accept correction; truth has perished and has been cut off from their mouth. Cut off your hair and cast it away, And take up a lamentation on the bare heights; For the Lord has rejected and forsaken The generation of His wrath." For the sons of Judah have done that which is evil in My sight,' declares the Lord, 'they have set their detestable things in the house which is called by My name, to defile it. They have built the high places of Topheth, which is in the valley of the son of Hinnom, to burn their sons and their daughters in the fire, which I did not command, and it did not come into My mind'" (Jer. 7:27-31).

Chapter Two

Lies and Not Truth Prevail in the Land

'Oh that my head were waters And my eyes a fountain of tears, That I might weep day and night For the slain of the daughter of my people! Oh that I had in the desert A wayfarers' lodging place; That I might leave my people And go from them! For all of them are adulterers, An assembly of treacherous men. They bend their tongue like their bow; Lies and not truth prevail in the land; For they proceed from evil to evil, And they do not know Me,' declares the Lord. 'Let everyone be on guard against his neighbor, And do not trust any brother; Because every brother deals craftily, And every neighbor goes about as a slanderer. Everyone deceives his neighbor And does not speak the truth, They have taught their tongue to speak lies; They weary themselves committing iniquity. Your dwelling is in the midst of deceit; Through deceit they refuse to know Me,' declares the Lord" (Jer. 9:1-6).

Speak My Word in Truth

'"I have heard what the prophets have said who prophesy falsely in My name, saying, "I had a dream, I had a dream!" How long? Is there anything in the hearts of the prophets who prophesy falsehood, even these prophets of the deception of their own heart, who intend to make My people forget My name by their dreams which they relate to one another, just as their fathers forgot My name because of Baal? "The prophet who has a dream may relate his dream, but let him who has My word speak My word in truth. What does straw have in common with grain?" declares the Lord. 'Is not My word like fire?' declares the Lord, and like a hammer which shatters a rock? 'Therefore behold, I am against the prophets,' declares the Lord, 'who steal My words from each other. "Behold, I am against the prophets,' declares the Lord, 'who use their tongues and declare, "The Lord declares." "Behold, I am against those who have prophesied false dreams,' declares the Lord, 'and related them and led My people astray by their falsehoods and reckless boasting; yet I did not send them or command them, nor do they furnish this people the slightest benefit,' declares the Lord" (Jer. 23:25-32).

I Will Reveal to Them an Abundance of Truth

"Then the word of the Lord came to Jeremiah the second time, while he was still confined in the court of the guard, saying, 'Thus says the Lord who made the earth, the Lord who formed it to establish it, the Lord is His name, "Call to Me and I will answer you, and I will tell you great and mighty things, which you do not know." For thus says the Lord God of Israel concerning the houses of this city, and concerning the houses of the kings of Judah which are broken down to make a defense against the siege ramps and against the sword, "While they are coming to fight with the Chaldeans and to fill them with the corpses of men whom I have slain in My anger and in My wrath, and I have hidden My face from this city because of all their wickedness: Behold, I will bring to it health and healing, and I will heal them; and I will reveal to them an abundance of peace and truth. 'I will restore the fortunes of Judah and the fortunes of Israel and will rebuild them as they were at first. I will cleanse them from all their iniquity by which they have sinned against Me, and I will pardon all their iniquities by which they have sinned against Me and by which they have transgressed against Me. It will be to Me a name of joy, praise and glory before all the nations of the earth which will hear of all the good that I do for them, and they will fear and tremble because of all the good and all the peace that I make for it'"" (Jer. 33:1-9).

It Will Fling Truth to the Ground

"Out of one of them came forth a rather small horn which grew exceedingly great toward the south, toward the east, and toward the Beautiful Land. It grew up to the host of heaven and caused some of the host and some of the stars to fall to the earth, and it trampled them down. It even magnified itself to be equal with the Commander of the host; and it removed the regular sacrifice from Him, and the place of His sanctuary was thrown down. And on account of transgression the host will be given over to the horn along with the regular sacrifice; and it will fling truth to the ground and perform its will and prosper. Then I heard a holy one speaking, and another holy one said to that particular one who was speaking, 'How long will the vision about the regular sacrifice apply, while the transgression causes horror, so as to allow both the holy place and the host to be trampled?' He said to me, 'For 2,300 evenings and mornings; then the holy place will be properly restored'" (Da. 8:9-14).

Giving Attention to Your Truth

"Righteousness belongs to You, O Lord, but to us open shame, as it is this day — to the men of Judah, the inhabitants of Jerusalem and all Israel, those who are nearby and those who are far away in all the countries to which You have driven them, because of their unfaithful deeds which they have committed against You. Open shame belongs to us, O Lord, to our kings, our princes and our fathers, because we have sinned against You. To the Lord our God belong compassion and forgiveness, for we have rebelled against Him; nor have we obeyed the voice of the Lord our God, to walk in His teachings which He set before us through His servants the prophets. Indeed all Israel has transgressed Your law and turned aside, not obeying Your voice; so the curse has been poured out on us, along with the oath which is written in the law of Moses the servant of God, for we have sinned against Him. Thus He has confirmed His words which He had spoken against us and against our rulers who ruled us, to bring on us great calamity; for under the whole heaven there has not been done anything like what was done to Jerusalem. As it is written in the law of Moses, all this calamity has come on us; yet we have not sought the favor of the Lord our God by turning from our iniquity and giving attention to Your truth. Therefore the Lord has kept the calamity in store and brought it on us; for the Lord our God is righteous with respect to all His deeds which He has done, but we have not obeyed His voice" (Da. 9:7-14).

What Is Inscribed in the Writing of Truth

"Then this one with human appearance touched me again and strengthened me. He said, O man of high esteem, do not be afraid. Peace be with you; take courage and be courageous!' Now as soon as he spoke to me, I received strength and said, 'May my lord speak, for you have strengthened me.' Then he said, 'Do you understand why I came to you? But I shall now return to fight against the prince of Persia; so

Chapter Two

I am going forth, and behold, the prince of Greece is about to come. However, I will tell you what is inscribed in the writing of truth. Yet there is no one who stands firmly with me against these forces except Michael your prince'" (Da. 10:18-21).

I Will Tell You the Truth

"In the first year of Darius the Mede, I arose to be an encouragement and a protection for him. And now I will tell you the truth. Behold, three more kings are going to arise in Persia. Then a fourth will gain far more riches than all of them; as soon as he becomes strong through his riches, he will arouse the whole empire against the realm of Greece. And a mighty king will arise, and he will rule with great authority and do as he pleases. But as soon as he has arisen, his kingdom will be broken up and parceled out toward the four points of the compass, though not to his own descendants, nor according to his authority which he wielded, for his sovereignty will be uprooted and given to others besides them" (Da. 11:1-4).

Give Truth to Jacob and Love to Abraham

"Shepherd Your people with Your scepter, The flock of Your possession Which dwells by itself in the woodland, In the midst of a fruitful field. Let them feed in Bashan and Gilead As in the days of old. As in the days when you came out from the land of Egypt, I will show you miracles. Nations will see and be ashamed Of all their might. They will put their hand on their mouth, Their ears will be deaf. They will lick the dust like a serpent, Like reptiles of the earth. They will come trembling out of their fortresses; To the Lord our God they will come in dread And they will be afraid before You. Who is a God like You, who pardons iniquity And passes over the rebellious act of the remnant of His possession? He does not retain His anger forever, Because He delights in unchanging love. He will again have compassion on us; He will tread our iniquities under foot. Yes, You will cast all their sins Into the depths of the sea. You will give truth to Jacob And unchanging love to Abraham, Which You swore to our forefathers From the days of old" (Mic. 7:14-20).

Jerusalem Will Be Called the City of Truth

"Then the word of the Lord of hosts came, saying, 'Thus says the Lord of hosts, "I am exceedingly jealous for Zion, yes, with great wrath I am jealous for her." Thus says the Lord, "I will return to Zion and will dwell in the midst of Jerusalem. Then Jerusalem will be called the City of Truth, and the mountain of the Lord of hosts will be called the Holy Mountain." Thus says the Lord of hosts, "Old men and old women will again sit in the streets of Jerusalem, each man with his staff in his hand because of age. And the streets of the city will be filled with boys and girls playing in its streets." Thus says the Lord of hosts, "If it is too difficult in the sight of the remnant of this people in those days, will it also be too difficult in My sight?" declares the Lord of hosts. Thus says the Lord of hosts, "Behold, I am going to save My people from the land of the east and from the land of the west; and I will bring them back and they will live in the midst of Jerusalem; and they shall be My people, and I will be their God in truth and righteousness'"" (Zec. 8:1-8).

Chapter Two

Speak the Truth to One Another

"For thus says the Lord of hosts, 'Just as I purposed to do harm to you when your fathers provoked Me to wrath,' says the Lord of hosts, 'and I have not relented, so I have again purposed in these days to do good to Jerusalem and to the house of Judah. Do not fear! These are the things which you should do: speak the truth to one another; judge with truth and judgment for peace in your gates. Also let none of you devise evil in your heart against another, and do not love perjury; for all these are what I hate,' declares the Lord" (Zec. 8:14-17).

Love Truth and Peace

"Then the word of the Lord of hosts came to me, saying, 'Thus says the Lord of hosts, "The fast of the fourth, the fast of the fifth, the fast of the seventh and the fast of the tenth months will become joy, gladness, and cheerful feasts for the house of Judah; so love truth and peace'"'" (Zec. 8:18-19).

Chapter Three

TRUTH IN THE NEW TESTAMENT

Teach the Way of God in Truth

"Then the Pharisees went and plotted together how they might trap Him in what He said. And they sent their disciples to Him, along with the Herodians, saying, 'Teacher, we know that You are truthful and teach the way of God in truth, and defer to no one; for You are not partial to any. Tell us then, what do You think? Is it lawful to give a poll-tax to Caesar, or not?' But Jesus perceived their malice, and said, 'Why are you testing Me, you hypocrites? Show Me the coin used for the poll-tax.' And they brought Him a denarius. And He said to them, 'Whose likeness and inscription is this?' They said to Him, 'Caesar's' Then He *said to them, 'Then render to Caesar the things that are Caesar's; and to God the things that are God's.' And hearing this, they were amazed, and leaving Him, they went away" (Mt. 22:15-22).

Told Him the Whole Truth

"A woman who had had a hemorrhage for twelve years, and had endured much at the hands of many physicians, and had spent all that she had and was not helped at all, but rather had grown worse —after hearing about Jesus, she came up in the crowd behind Him and touched His cloak. For she thought, 'If I just touch His garments, I will get well.' Immediately the flow of her blood was dried up; and she felt in her body that she was healed of her affliction. Immediately Jesus, perceiving in Himself that the power proceeding from Him had gone forth, turned around in the crowd and said, 'Who touched My garments?' And His disciples said to Him, 'You see the crowd pressing in on You, and You say, "Who touched

Me?'" And He looked around to see the woman who had done this. But the woman fearing and trembling, aware of what had happened to her, came and fell down before Him and told Him the whole truth. And He said to her, "Daughter, your faith has made you well; go in peace and be healed of your affliction'" (Mr. 5:25-34).

Teach the Way of God in Truth

"Then they sent some of the Pharisees and Herodians to Him in order to trap Him in a statement. They came and said to Him, 'Teacher, we know that You are truthful and defer to no one; for You are not partial to any, but teach the way of God in truth. Is it lawful to pay a poll-tax to Caesar, or not? Shall we pay or shall we not pay?' But He, knowing their hypocrisy, said to them, 'Why are you testing Me? Bring Me a denarius to look at.' They brought one. And He said to them, 'Whose likeness and inscription is this?' And they said to Him, "Caesar's.' And Jesus said to them, 'Render to Caesar the things that are Caesar's, and to God the things that are God's.' And they were amazed at Him" (Mr. 12:13-17).

The Exact Truth About Things

"Inasmuch as many have undertaken to compile an account of the things accomplished among us, just as they were handed down to us by those who from the beginning were eyewitnesses and servants of the word, it seemed fitting for me as well, having investigated everything carefully from the beginning, to write it out for you in consecutive order, most excellent Theophilus; so that you may know the exact truth about the things you have been taught" (Lk.. 1:1-4).

Chapter Three

I Say to You in Truth

"And He said, 'Truly I say to you, no prophet is welcome in his hometown. But I say to you in truth, there were many widows in Israel in the days of Elijah, when the sky was shut up for three years and six months, when a great famine came over all the land; and yet Elijah was sent to none of them, but only to Zarephath, in the land of Sidon, to a woman who was a widow. And there were many lepers in Israel in the time of Elisha the prophet; and none of them was cleansed, but only Naaman the Syrian.' And all the people in the synagogue were filled with rage as they heard these things; and they got up and drove Him out of the city, and led Him to the brow of the hill on which their city had been built, in order to throw Him down the cliff. But passing through their midst, He went His way" (Lu. 4:24-30).

In Truth

"The scribes and the chief priests tried to lay hands on Him that very hour, and they feared the people; for they understood that He spoke this parable against them. So they watched Him, and sent spies who pretended to be righteous, in order that they might catch Him in some statement, so that they could deliver Him to the rule and the authority of the governor. They questioned Him, saying, 'Teacher, we know that You speak and teach correctly, and You are not partial to any, but teach the way of God in truth. Is it lawful for us to pay taxes to Caesar, or not? But He detected their trickery and said to them, 'Show Me a denarius. Whose likeness and inscription does it have?' They said, 'Caesar's.' And He said to them, 'Then render to Caesar the things that are Caesar's, and to God the things that are God's.' And they were unable to catch

Him in a saying in the presence of the people; and being amazed at His answer, they became silent" (Lu. 20:19-26).

Full of Grace and Truth

"And the Word became flesh, and dwelt among us, and we saw His glory, glory as of the only begotten from the Father, full of grace and truth. John testified about Him and cried out, saying, 'This was He of whom I said, "He who comes after me has a higher rank than I, for He existed before me.'" For of His fullness we have all received, and grace upon grace. For the Law was given through Moses; grace and truth were realized through Jesus Christ" (Jn. 1:14-17).

He Who Practices the Truth Comes to the Light

"For God so loved the world, that He gave His only begotten Son, that whoever believes in Him shall not perish, but have eternal life. For God did not send the Son into the world to judge the world, but that the world might be saved through Him. He who believes in Him is not judged; he who does not believe has been judged already, because he has not believed in the name of the only begotten Son of God. This is the judgment, that the Light has come into the world, and men loved the darkness rather than the Light, for their deeds were evil. For everyone who does evil hates the Light, and does not come to the Light for fear that his deeds will be exposed. But he who practices the truth comes to the Light, so that his deeds may be manifested as having been wrought in God" (Jn. 3:16-21).

Chapter Three

Will Worship the Father in Spirit and Truth

"The woman said to Him, 'Sir, give me this water, so I will not be thirsty nor come all the way here to draw.' He said to her, 'Go, call your husband and come here." The woman answered and said, 'I have no husband.' Jesus said to her, 'You have correctly said, "I have no husband"; for you have had five husbands, and the one whom you now have is not your husband; this you have said truly." The woman said to Him, 'Sir, I perceive that You are a prophet. Our fathers worshiped in this mountain, and you people say that in Jerusalem is the place where men ought to worship.' Jesus said to her, 'Woman, believe Me, an hour is coming when neither in this mountain nor in Jerusalem will you worship the Father. You worship what you do not know; we worship what we know, for salvation is from the Jews. But an hour is coming, and now is, when the true worshipers will worship the Father in spirit and truth; for such people the Father seeks to be His worshipers. God is spirit, and those who worship Him must worship in spirit and truth.' The woman said to Him, 'I know that Messiah is coming (He who is called Christ); when that One comes, He will declare all things to us.' Jesus said to her, 'I who speak to you am He'" (Jn. 4:15-26).

He Has Testified to the Truth

"If I alone testify about Myself, My testimony is not true. There is another who testifies of Me, and I know that the testimony which He gives about Me is true. You have sent to John, and he has testified to the truth. But the testimony which I receive is not from man, but I say these things so that you may be saved. He was the lamp that was burning and was shining and you were willing to rejoice for a while in his light. But the testimony which I have is greater than the testimony of John; for the works which the Father has given Me to accomplish — the very works that I do — testify about Me, that the Father has sent Me. And the Father who sent Me, He has testified of Me. You have neither heard His voice at any time nor seen His form. You do not have His word abiding in you, for you do not believe Him whom He sent. You search the Scriptures because you think that in them you have eternal life; it is these that testify about Me; and you are unwilling to come to Me so that you may have life. I do not receive glory from men; but I know you, that you do not have the love of God in yourselves. I have come in My Father's name, and you do not receive Me; if another comes in his own name, you will receive him. How can you believe, when you receive glory from one another and you do not seek the glory that is from the one and only God? Do not think that I will accuse you before the Father; the one who accuses you is Moses, in whom you have set your hope. For if you believed Moses, you would believe Me, for he wrote about Me. But if you do not believe his writings, how will you believe My words" (Jn. 5:31-47)?

The Truth Will Make You Free

"So Jesus was saying to those Jews who had believed Him, 'If you continue in My word, then you are truly disciples of Mine; and you will know the truth, and the truth will make you free.' They answered Him, 'We are Abraham's descendants and have never yet been enslaved to anyone; how is it that You say, "You will become free"'" (Jn. 8:31-33)?

A Man Who Has Told You the Truth

"They answered and said to Him, 'Abraham is our father.' Jesus said to them, 'If you are Abraham's children, do the deeds of Abraham. But as it is, you are seeking to kill Me, a man who has told you the truth, which I heard from God; this Abraham did not do. You are doing the deeds of your father.' They said to Him, 'We were not born of fornication; we have one Father: God.' Jesus said to them, 'If God were your Father, you would love Me, for I proceeded forth and have come from God, for I have not even come on My own initiative, but He sent Me. Why do you not understand what I am saying? It is because you cannot hear My word. You are of your father the devil, and you want to do the desires of your father. He was a murderer from the beginning, and does not stand in the truth because there is no truth in him. Whenever he speaks a lie, he speaks from his own nature, for he is a liar and the father of lies. But because I speak the truth, you do not believe Me. Which one of you convicts Me of sin? If I speak truth, why do you not believe Me? He who is of God hears the words of God; for this reason you do not hear them, because you are not of God'" (Jn. 8:39-47).

I Am the Way, and the Truth, and the Life

"Do not let your heart be troubled; believe in God, believe also in Me. In My Father's house are many dwelling places; if it were not so, I would have told you; for I go to prepare a place for you. If I go and prepare a place for you, I will come again and receive you to Myself, that where I am, there you may be also. And you know the way where I am going. Thomas said to Him, 'Lord, we do not know where You are going, how do we know the way?' Jesus said to him, 'I am the way, and the truth, and the life; no one comes to the Father but through Me. If you had known Me, you would have known My Father also; from now on you know Him, and have seen Him'" (Jn. 14:1-7).

The Spirit of Truth

"If you love Me, you will keep My commandments. I will ask the Father, and He will give you another Helper, that He may be with you forever; that is the Spirit of truth, whom the world cannot receive, because it does not see Him or know Him, but you know Him because He abides with you and will be in you" (Jn. 14:15-17).

The Helper, the Spirit of Truth Who Proceeds from the Father

"When the Helper comes, whom I will send to you from the Father, that is the Spirit of truth who proceeds from the Father, He will testify about Me, and you will testify also, because you have been with Me from the beginning" (Jn. 15:26-27).

I Tell You the Truth, It Is to Your Advantage

"But now I am going to Him who sent Me; and none of you asks Me, "Where are You going?" But because I have said these things to you, sorrow has filled your heart. But I tell you the truth, it is to your advantage that I go away; for if I do not go away, the Helper will not come to you; but if I go, I will send Him to you. And He, when He comes, will convict the world concerning sin and righteousness and judgment; concerning sin, because they do not believe in Me; and concerning righteousness, because I go to the Father and you no longer see Me; and concerning judgment, because the ruler of this world has been judged" (Jn. 16:5-11).

But When He, the Spirit of Truth, Comes

"I have many more things to say to you, but you cannot bear them now. But when He, the Spirit of truth, comes, He will guide you into all the truth; for He will not speak on His own initiative, but whatever He hears, He will speak; and He will disclose to you what is to come. He will glorify Me, for He will take of Mine and will disclose it to you. All things that the Father has are Mine; therefore I said that He takes of Mine and will disclose it to you" (Jn. 16:12-15).

Sanctify Them in the Truth

"But now I come to You; and these things I speak in the world so that they may have My joy made full in themselves. I have given them Your word; and the world has hated them, because they are not of the world, even as I am not of the world. I do not ask You to take them out of the world, but to keep them from the evil one. They are not of the world, even as I am not of the world. Sanctify them in the truth; Your word is truth. As You sent Me into the world, I also have sent them into the world. For their sakes I sanctify Myself, that they themselves also may be sanctified in truth" (Jn. 17:13-19).

Everyone Who Is of the Truth Hears My Voice

"Therefore Pilate entered again into the Praetorium, and summoned Jesus and said to Him, 'Are You the King of the Jews?' Jesus answered, 'Are you saying this on your own initiative, or did others tell you about Me?' Pilate answered, 'I am not a Jew, am I? Your own nation and the chief priests delivered You to me; what have You done?' Jesus answered, 'My kingdom is not of this world. If My kingdom were of this world, then My servants would be fighting so that I would not be handed over to the Jews; but as it is, My kingdom is not of this realm.' Therefore Pilate said to Him, 'So You are a king?' Jesus answered, 'You say correctly that I am a king. For this I have been born, and for this I have come into the world, to testify to the truth. Everyone who is of the truth hears My voice.' Pilate said to Him, 'What is truth?' And when he had said this, he went out again to the Jews and said to them, 'I find no guilt in Him'" (Jn. 18:33-38).

He Is Telling the Truth

"Then the Jews, because it was the day of preparation, so that the bodies would not remain on the cross on the Sabbath (for that Sabbath was a high day), asked Pilate that their legs might be broken, and that they might be taken away. So the soldiers came, and broke the legs of the first man and of the other who was crucified with Him; but coming to Jesus, when they saw that He was already dead, they did not break His legs. But one of the soldiers pierced His side with a spear, and immediately blood and water came out. And he who has seen has testified, and his testimony is true; and he knows that he is telling the truth, so that you also may believe. For these things came to pass to fulfill the Scripture, 'NOT A BONE OF HIM SHALL BE BROKEN.' And again another Scripture says, 'THEY SHALL LOOK ON HIM WHOM THEY PIERCED'" (Jn. 19:31-37).

Chapter Three

I Utter Words of Sober Truth

"While Paul was saying this in his defense, Festus *said in a loud voice, 'Paul, you are out of your mind! Your great learning is driving you mad.' But Paul said, 'I am not out of my mind, most excellent Festus, but I utter words of sober truth. For the king knows about these matters, and I speak to him also with confidence, since I am persuaded that none of these things escape his notice; for this has not been done in a corner. King Agrippa, do you believe the Prophets? I know that you do.' Agrippa replied to Paul, 'In a short time you will persuade me to become a Christian.' And Paul said, 'I would wish to God, that whether in a short or long time, not only you, but also all who hear me this day, might become such as I am, except for these chains'" (Ac. 26:24-29).

Men Who Suppress the Truth in Unrighteousness

"For the wrath of God is revealed from heaven against all ungodliness and unrighteousness of men who suppress the truth in unrighteousness, because that which is known about God is evident within them; for God made it evident to them. For since the creation of the world His invisible attributes, His eternal power and divine nature, have been clearly seen, being understood through what has been made, so that they are without excuse. For even though they knew God, they did not honor Him as God or give thanks, but they became futile in their speculations, and their foolish heart was darkened. Professing to be wise, they became fools, and exchanged the glory of the incorruptible God for an image in the form of corruptible man and of birds and four-footed animals and crawling creatures" (Ro 1:18-23).

Chapter Three

They Exchanged the Truth of God for a Lie

"Therefore God gave them over in the lusts of their hearts to impurity, so that their bodies would be dishonored among them. For they exchanged the truth of God for a lie, and worshiped and served the creature rather than the Creator, who is blessed forever. Amen" (Ro. 1:24-25).

Selfishly Ambitious and Do Not Obey the Truth

"Therefore you have no excuse, everyone of you who passes judgment, for in that which you judge another, you condemn yourself; for you who judge practice the same things. And we know that the judgment of God rightly falls upon those who practice such things. But do you suppose this, O man, when you pass judgment on those who practice such things and do the same yourself, that you will escape the judgment of God? Or do you think lightly of the riches of His kindness and tolerance and patience, not knowing that the kindness of God leads you to repentance? But because of your stubbornness and unrepentant heart you are storing up wrath for yourself in the day of wrath and revelation of the righteous judgment of God, who WILL RENDER TO EACH PERSON ACCORDING TO HIS DEEDS: to those who by perseverance in doing good seek for glory and honor and immortality, eternal life; but to those who are selfishly ambitious and do not obey the truth, but obey unrighteousness, wrath and indignation. There will be tribulation and distress for every soul of man who does evil, of the Jew first and also of the Greek, but glory and honor and peace to everyone who does good, to the Jew first and also to the Greek. For there is no partiality with God" (Ro. 2:1-11).

Chapter Three

The Embodiment of Knowledge and of the Truth

"But if you bear the name 'Jew' and rely upon the Law and boast in God, and know His will and approve the things that are essential, being instructed out of the Law, and are confident that you yourself are a guide to the blind, a light to those who are in darkness, a corrector of the foolish, a teacher of the immature, having in the Law the embodiment of knowledge and of the truth, you, therefore, who teach another, do you not teach yourself? You who preach that one shall not steal, do you steal? You who say that one should not commit adultery, do you commit adultery? You who abhor idols, do you rob temples? You who boast in the Law, through your breaking the Law, do you dishonor God? For 'THE NAME OF GOD IS BLASPHEMED AMONG THE GENTILES BECAUSE OF YOU,' just as it is written" (Ro. 2:17-24).

He Truth of God Abounded to His Glory

"Then what advantage has the Jew? Or what is the benefit of circumcision? Great in every respect. First of all, that they were entrusted with the oracles of God. What then? If some did not believe, their unbelief will not nullify the faithfulness of God, will it? May it never be! Rather, let God be found true, though every man be found a liar, as it is written, 'THAT YOU MAY BE JUSTIFIED IN YOUR WORDS, AND PREVAIL WHEN YOU ARE JUDGED.' But if our unrighteousness demonstrates the righteousness of God, what shall we say? The God who inflicts wrath is not unrighteous, is He? (I am speaking in human terms.) May it never be! For otherwise, how will God judge the world? But if through my lie the truth of God abounded to His glory, why am I also still being judged as a sinner? And why not say (as we are slanderously reported and as some claim that we say), 'Let us do evil that good may come'? Their condemnation is just" (Ro. 3:1-8).

I Am Telling the Truth in Christ

"I am telling the truth in Christ, I am not lying, my conscience testifies with me in the Holy Spirit, that I have great sorrow and unceasing grief in my heart. For I could wish that I myself were accursed, separated from Christ for the sake of my brethren, my kinsmen according to the flesh, who are Israelites, to whom belongs the adoption as sons, and the glory and the covenants and the giving of the Law and the temple service and the promises, whose are the fathers, and from whom is the Christ according to the flesh, who is over all, God blessed forever. Amen" (Ro. 9:1-5).

On Behalf of the Truth of God

"Therefore, accept one another, just as Christ also accepted us to the glory of God. For I say that Christ has become a servant to the circumcision on behalf of the truth of God to confirm the promises given to the fathers, and for the Gentiles to glorify God for His mercy; as it is written, 'THEREFORE I WILL GIVE PRAISE TO YOU AMONG THE GENTILES, AND I WILL SING TO YOUR NAME.' Again he says, 'REJOICE, O GENTILES, WITH HIS PEOPLE.' And again, 'PRAISE THE LORD ALL YOU GENTILES, AND LET ALL THE PEOPLES PRAISE HIM." Again Isaiah says, 'THERE SHALL COME THE ROOT OF JESSE, AND HE WHO ARISES TO RULE OVER THE GENTILES, IN HIM SHALL THE GENTILES HOPE.' Now may the God of hope fill you with all joy and peace in believing, so that you will abound in hope by the power of the Holy Spirit" (Ro. 15:7-13).

Chapter Three

With the Unleavened Bread of Sincerity and Truth

"Your boasting is not good. Do you not know that a little leaven leavens the whole lump of dough? Clean out the old leaven so that you may be a new lump, just as you are in fact unleavened. For Christ our Passover also has been sacrificed. Therefore let us celebrate the feast, not with old leaven, nor with the leaven of malice and wickedness, but with the unleavened bread of sincerity and truth" (1Co. 5:6-8).

Rejoices with the Truth

"Love is patient, love is kind and is not jealous; love does not brag and is not arrogant, does not act unbecomingly; it does not seek its own, is not provoked, does not take into account a wrong suffered, does not rejoice in unrighteousness, but rejoices with the truth; bears all things, believes all things, hopes all things, endures all things" (1Co. 13:4-7).

By the Manifestation of Truth

"Therefore, since we have this ministry, as we received mercy, we do not lose heart, but we have renounced the things hidden because of shame, not walking in craftiness or adulterating the word of God, but by the manifestation of truth commending ourselves to every man's conscience in the sight of God. And even if our gospel is veiled, it is veiled to those who are perishing, in whose case the god of this world has blinded the minds of the unbelieving so that they might not see the light of the gospel of the glory of Christ, who is the image of God. For we do not preach ourselves but Christ Jesus as Lord, and ourselves as your bond-servants for Jesus' sake. For

God, who said, 'Light shall shine out of darkness,' is the One who has shone in our hearts to give the Light of the knowledge of the glory of God in the face of Christ" (2Co.4:1-6).

In the Word of Truth

"And working together with Him, we also urge you not to receive the grace of God in vain —for He says, 'AT THE ACCEPTABLE TIME I LISTENED TO YOU, AND ON THE DAY OF SALVATION I HELPED YOU.' Behold, now is 'THE ACCEPTABLE TIME,' behold, now is 'THE DAY OF SALVATION' — giving no cause for offense in anything, so that the ministry will not be discredited, but in everything commending ourselves as servants of God, in much endurance, in afflictions, in hardships, in distresses, in beatings, in imprisonments, in tumults, in labors, in sleeplessness, in hunger, in purity, in knowledge, in patience, in kindness, in the Holy Spirit, in genuine love, in the word of truth, in the power of God; by the weapons of righteousness for the right hand and the left, by glory and dishonor, by evil report and good report; regarded as deceivers and yet true; as unknown yet well-known, as dying yet behold, we live; as punished yet not put to death, as sorrowful yet always rejoicing, as poor yet making many rich, as having nothing yet possessing all things" (2Co. 6:1-10).

We Spoke All Things to You in Truth

"For even when we came into Macedonia our flesh had no rest, but we were afflicted on every side: conflicts without, fears within. But God, who comforts the depressed, comforted us by the coming of Titus; and not only by his coming, but also by the comfort with which he was comforted in you, as he reported to us your longing, your mourning, your zeal for me; so that I rejoiced even more. For though I caused you sorrow by my letter, I do not regret it; though I did regret it — for I see that that letter caused you sorrow, though only for a while —I now rejoice, not that you were made sorrowful, but that you were made sorrowful to the point of repentance; for you were made sorrowful according to the will of God, so that you might not suffer loss in anything through us. For the sorrow that is according to the will of God produces a repentance without regret, leading to salvation, but the sorrow of the world produces death. For behold what earnestness this very thing, this godly sorrow, has produced in you: what vindication of yourselves, what indignation, what fear, what longing, what zeal, what avenging of wrong! In everything you demonstrated yourselves to be innocent in the matter. So although I wrote to you, it was not for the sake of the offender nor for the sake of the one offended, but that your earnestness on our behalf might be made known to you in the sight of God. For this reason we have been comforted. And besides our comfort, we rejoiced even much more for the joy of Titus, because his spirit has been refreshed by you all. For if in anything I have boasted to him about you, I was not put to shame; but as we spoke all things to you in truth, so also our boasting before Titus proved to be the truth. His affection abounds all the more toward you, as he remembers the obedience of you all, how you received him with fear and trembling. I rejoice that in everything I have confidence in you" (2Co. 7:5-16).

The Truth of Christ Is in Me

"Or did I commit a sin in humbling myself so that you might be exalted, because I preached the gospel of

God to you without charge? I robbed other churches by taking wages from them to serve you; and when I was present with you and was in need, I was not a burden to anyone; for when the brethren came from Macedonia they fully supplied my need, and in everything I kept myself from being a burden to you, and will continue to do so. As the truth of Christ is in me, this boasting of mine will not be stopped in the regions of Achaia. Why? Because I do not love you? God knows I do" (2Co. 11:7-11)!

I Will Be Speaking the Truth

"Boasting is necessary, though it is not profitable; but I will go on to visions and revelations of the Lord. I know a man in Christ who fourteen years ago — whether in the body I do not know, or out of the body I do not know, God knows — such a man was caught up to the third heaven. And I know how such a man — whether in the body or apart from the body I do not know, God knows —was caught up into Paradise and heard inexpressible words, which a man is not permitted to speak. On behalf of such a man I will boast; but on my own behalf I will not boast, except in regard to my weaknesses. For if I do wish to boast I will not be foolish, for I will be speaking the truth; but I refrain from this, so that no one will credit me with more than he sees in me or hears from me. Because of the surpassing greatness of the revelations, for this reason, to keep me from exalting myself, there was given me a thorn in the flesh, a messenger of Satan to torment me — to keep me from exalting myself! Concerning this I implored the Lord three times that it might leave me. And He has said to me, 'My grace is sufficient for you, for power is perfected in weakness.' Most gladly, therefore, I will rather boast about my weaknesses, so that the power of Christ may dwell in me. Therefore I am well content with weaknesses, with insults, with distresses, with persecutions, with difficulties, for Christ's sake; for when I am weak, then I am strong" (2Co. 12:1-10).

We Can Do Nothing Against the Truth

"Test yourselves to see if you are in the faith; examine yourselves! Or do you not recognize this about yourselves, that Jesus Christ is in you — unless indeed you fail the test? But I trust that you will realize that we ourselves do not fail the test. Now we pray to God that you do no wrong; not that we ourselves may appear approved, but that you may do what is right, even though we may appear unapproved. For we can do nothing against the truth, but only for the truth. For we rejoice when we ourselves are weak but you are strong; this we also pray for, that you be made complete. For this reason I am writing these things while absent, so that when present I need not use severity, in accordance with the authority which the Lord gave me for building up and not for tearing down" (2Co. 13:5-10).

So That the Truth of the Gospel Would Remain

"Then after an interval of fourteen years I went up again to Jerusalem with Barnabas, taking Titus along also. It was because of a revelation that I went up; and I submitted to them the gospel which I preach among the Gentiles, but I did so in private to those who were of reputation, for fear that I might be running, or had run, in vain. But not even Titus, who was with me, though he was a Greek, was compelled to be circumcised. But it was because of the false brethren secretly brought in, who had sneaked in to spy out our liberty which we have in Christ

Jesus, in order to bring us into bondage. But we did not yield in subjection to them for even an hour, so that the truth of the gospel would remain with you. But from those who were of high reputation (what they were makes no difference to me; God shows no partiality) — well, those who were of reputation contributed nothing to me. But on the contrary, seeing that I had been entrusted with the gospel to the uncircumcised, just as Peter had been to the circumcised (for He who effectually worked for Peter in his apostleship to the circumcised effectually worked for me also to the Gentiles), and recognizing the grace that had been given to me, James and Cephas and John, who were reputed to be pillars, gave to me and Barnabas the right hand of fellowship, so that we might go to the Gentiles and they to the circumcised. They only asked us to remember the poor — the very thing I also was eager to do" (Gal. 2:1-10).

Straightforward About the Truth of the Gospel

"But when Cephas came to Antioch, I opposed him to his face, because he stood condemned. For prior to the coming of certain men from James, he used to eat with the Gentiles; but when they came, he began to withdraw and hold himself aloof, fearing the party of the circumcision. The rest of the Jews joined him in hypocrisy, with the result that even Barnabas was carried away by their hypocrisy. But when I saw that they were not straightforward about the truth of the gospel, I said to Cephas in the presence of all, 'If you, being a Jew, live like the Gentiles and not like the Jews, how is it that you compel the Gentiles to live like Jews'" (Gal. 2:11-14)?

Chapter Three

I Become Your Enemy by Telling You the Truth?

"I beg of you, brethren, become as I am, for I also have become as you are. You have done me no wrong; but you know that it was because of a bodily illness that I preached the gospel to you the first time; and that which was a trial to you in my bodily condition you did not despise or loathe, but you received me as an angel of God, as Christ Jesus Himself. Where then is that sense of blessing you had? For I bear you witness that, if possible, you would have plucked out your eyes and given them to me. So have I become your enemy by telling you the truth? They eagerly seek you, not commendably, but they wish to shut you out so that you will seek them. But it is good always to be eagerly sought in a commendable manner, and not only when I am present with you. My children, with whom I am again in labor until Christ is formed in you — but I could wish to be present with you now and to change my tone, for I am perplexed about you" (Gal. 4:12-20).

Who Hindered You from Obeying the Truth?

"You were running well; who hindered you from obeying the truth? This persuasion did not come from Him who calls you. A little leaven leavens the whole lump of dough. I have confidence in you in the Lord that you will adopt no other view; but the one who is disturbing you will bear his judgment, whoever he is. But I, brethren, if I still preach circumcision, why am I still persecuted? Then the stumbling block of the cross has been abolished. I wish that those who are troubling you would even mutilate themselves" (Gal. 5:7-12).

Chapter Three

After Listening to the Message of Truth

"Blessed be the God and Father of our Lord Jesus Christ, who has blessed us with every spiritual blessing in the heavenly places in Christ, just as He chose us in Him before the foundation of the world, that we would be holy and blameless before Him. In love He predestined us to adoption as sons through Jesus Christ to Himself, according to the kind intention of His will, to the praise of the glory of His grace, which He freely bestowed on us in the Beloved. In Him we have redemption through His blood, the forgiveness of our trespasses, according to the riches of His grace which He lavished on us. In all wisdom and insight He made known to us the mystery of His will, according to His kind intention which He purposed in Him with a view to an administration suitable to the fullness of the times, that is, the summing up of all things in Christ, things in the heavens and things on the earth. In Him also we have obtained an inheritance, having been predestined according to His purpose who works all things after the counsel of His will, to the end that we who were the first to hope in Christ would be to the praise of His glory. In Him, you also, after listening to the message of truth, the gospel of your salvation — having also believed, you were sealed in Him with the Holy Spirit of promise, who is given as a pledge of our inheritance, with a view to the redemption of God's own possession, to the praise of His glory" (Eph. 1:3-14).

Speaking the Truth in Love

"Therefore I, the prisoner of the Lord, implore you to walk in a manner worthy of the calling with which you have been called, with all humility and gentleness, with patience, showing tolerance for one another in love, being diligent to preserve the unity of the Spirit in the bond of peace. There is one body and one Spirit, just as also you were called in one hope of your calling; one Lord, one faith, one baptism, one God and Father of all who is over all and through all and in all. But to each one of us grace was given according to the measure of Christ's gift. Therefore it says, 'WHEN HE ASCENDED ON HIGH, HE LED CAPTIVE A HOST OF CAPTIVES, AND HE GAVE GIFTS TO MEN.' (Now this expression, 'He ascended,' what does it mean except that He also had descended into the lower parts of the earth? He who descended is Himself also He who ascended far above all the heavens, so that He might fill all things.) And He gave some as apostles, and some as prophets, and some as evangelists, and some as pastors and teachers, for the equipping of the saints for the work of service, to the building up of the body of Christ; until we all attain to the unity of the faith, and of the knowledge of the Son of God, to a mature man, to the measure of the stature which belongs to the fullness of Christ. As a result, we are no longer to be children, tossed here and there by waves and carried about by every wind of doctrine, by the trickery of men, by craftiness in deceitful scheming; but speaking the truth in love, we are to grow up in all aspects into Him who is the head, even Christ, from whom the whole body, being fitted and held together by what every joint supplies, according to the proper working of each individual part, causes the growth of the body for the building up of itself in love" (Eph. 4:1-16).

Just as Truth Is in Jesus

"So this I say, and affirm together with the Lord, that you walk no longer just as the Gentiles also walk, in the futility of their mind, being darkened in their understanding, excluded from the life of God because of the ignorance that is in them, because of the hardness of their heart; and they, having become callous, have given themselves over to sensuality for the practice of every kind of impurity with greediness. But you did not learn Christ in this way, if indeed you have heard Him and have been taught in Him, just as truth is in Jesus, that, in reference to your former manner of life, you lay aside the old self, which is being corrupted in accordance with the lusts of deceit, and that you be renewed in the spirit of your mind, and put on the new self, which in the likeness of God has been created in righteousness and holiness of the truth" (Eph. 4:17-24).

Speak Truth Each One of You

"Therefore, laying aside falsehood, SPEAK TRUTH EACH ONE of you WITH HIS NEIGHBOR, for we are members of one another. BE ANGRY, AND yet DO NOT SIN; do not let the sun go down on your anger, and do not give the devil an opportunity. He who steals must steal no longer; but rather he must labor, performing with his own hands what is good, so that he will have something to share with one who has need. Let no unwholesome word proceed from your mouth, but only such a word as is good for edification according to the need of the moment, so that it will give grace to those who hear. Do not grieve the Holy Spirit of God, by whom you were sealed for the day of redemption. Let all bitterness and wrath and anger and clamor and slander be put away from you, along with all malice. Be kind to one another, tender-hearted, forgiving each other, just as God in Christ also has forgiven you" (Eph. 4:25-32).

Chapter Three

Consists in all Goodness and Righteousness and Truth

"Let no one deceive you with empty words, for because of these things the wrath of God comes upon the sons of disobedience. Therefore do not be partakers with them; for you were formerly darkness, but now you are Light in the Lord; walk as children of Light (for the fruit of the Light consists in all goodness and righteousness and truth), trying to learn what is pleasing to the Lord. Do not participate in the unfruitful deeds of darkness, but instead even expose them; for it is disgraceful even to speak of the things which are done by them in secret. But all things become visible when they are exposed by the light, for everything that becomes visible is light. For this reason it says, 'Awake, sleeper, And arise from the dead, And Christ will shine on you'" (Eph. 5:6-14).

Having Girded Your Loins with Truth

"Finally, be strong in the Lord and in the strength of His might. Put on the full armor of God, so that you will be able to stand firm against the schemes of the devil. For our struggle is not against flesh and blood, but against the rulers, against the powers, against the world forces of this darkness, against the spiritual forces of wickedness in the heavenly places. Therefore, take up the full armor of God, so that you will be able to resist in the evil day, and having done everything, to stand firm. Stand firm therefore, HAVING GIRDED YOUR LOINS WITH TRUTH, and HAVING PUT ON THE BREASTPLATE OF RIGHTEOUSNESS, and having shod YOUR FEET WITH THE PREPARATION OF THE GOSPEL OF PEACE; in addition to all, taking up the shield of faith with which you will be able to extinguish all the flaming arrows of the evil one. And take THE HELMET OF SALVATION, and the sword of the Spirit, which is the word of God" (Eph. 6:10-17).

In Pretense or in Truth

"Now I want you to know, brethren, that my circumstances have turned out for the greater progress of the gospel, so that my imprisonment in the cause of Christ has become well known throughout the whole praetorian guard and to everyone else, and that most of the brethren, trusting in the Lord because of my imprisonment, have far more courage to speak the word of God without fear. Some, to be sure, are preaching Christ even from envy and strife, but some also from good will; the latter do it out of love, knowing that I am appointed for the defense of the gospel; the former proclaim Christ out of selfish ambition rather than from pure motives, thinking to cause me distress in my imprisonment. What then? Only that in every way, whether in pretense or in truth, Christ is proclaimed; and in this I rejoice. Yes, and I will rejoice, for I know that this will turn out for my deliverance through your prayers and the provision of the Spirit of Jesus Christ, according to my earnest expectation and hope, that I will not be put to shame in anything, but that with all boldness, Christ will even now, as always, be exalted in my body, whether by life or by death" (Php. 1:12-20).

You Previously Heard in the Word of Truth

"We give thanks to God, the Father of our Lord Jesus Christ, praying always for you, since we heard of your faith in Christ Jesus and the love which you have for all the saints; because of the hope laid up for you in heaven, of which you previously heard in the word of truth, the gospel which has come to you, just as in all the world also it is constantly bearing fruit and increasing, even as it has been doing in you also since the day you heard of it and understood the grace of God in truth; just as you learned it from Epaphras, our beloved fellow bond-servant, who is a faithful servant of Christ on our behalf, and he also informed us of your love in the Spirit" (Col. 1:3-8).

They Did Not Receive the Love of the Truth

"Now we request you, brethren, with regard to the coming of our Lord Jesus Christ and our gathering together to Him, that you not be quickly shaken from your composure or be disturbed either by a spirit or a message or a letter as if from us, to the effect that the day of the Lord has come. Let no one in any way deceive you, for it will not come unless the apostasy comes first, and the man of lawlessness is revealed, the son of destruction, who opposes and exalts himself above every so-called god or object of worship, so that he takes his seat in the temple of God, displaying himself as being God. Do you not remember that while I was still with you, I was telling you these things? And you know what restrains him now, so that in his time he will be revealed. For the mystery of lawlessness is already at work; only he who now restrains will do so until he is taken out of the way. Then that lawless one will be revealed whom the Lord will slay with the breath of His mouth and bring to an end by the appearance of His coming; that is, the one whose coming is in accord with the activity of Satan, with all power and signs and false wonders, and with all the deception of wickedness for those who perish, because they did not receive the love of the truth so as to be saved. For this reason God will send upon them a deluding influence so that they will believe what is false, in order that they all may be judged who did not believe the truth, but took pleasure in wickedness" (2Th. 2:1-12).

Sanctification by the Spirit and Faith in the Truth

"But we should always give thanks to God for you, brethren beloved by the Lord, because God has chosen you from the beginning for salvation through sanctification by the Spirit and faith in the truth. It was for this He called you through our gospel, that you may gain the glory of our Lord Jesus Christ. So then, brethren, stand firm and hold to the traditions which you were taught, whether by word of mouth or by letter from us" (2Th. 2:13-15).

To Come to the Knowledge of the Truth

"First of all, then, I urge that entreaties and prayers, petitions and thanksgivings, be made on behalf of all men, for kings and all who are in authority, so that we may lead a tranquil and quiet life in all godliness and dignity. This is good and acceptable in the sight of God our Savior, who desires all men to be saved and to come to the knowledge of the truth. For there is one God, and one mediator also between God and men, the man Christ Jesus, who gave Himself as a ransom for all, the testimony given at the proper time. For this I was appointed a preacher and an apostle (I am telling the truth, I am not lying) as a teacher of the Gentiles in faith and truth" (1Ti. 2:1-7).

The Pillar and Support of the Truth

"I am writing these things to you, hoping to come to you before long; but in case I am delayed, I write so that you will know how one ought to conduct himself in the household of God, which is the church of the living God, the pillar and support of the truth. By common confession, great is the mystery of godliness: He who was revealed in the flesh, Was vindicated in the Spirit, Seen by angels, Proclaimed among the nations, Believed on in the world, Taken up in glory" (1Ti. 3:14-16).

Those Who Believe and Know the Truth

"But the Spirit explicitly says that in later times some will fall away from the faith, paying attention to deceitful spirits and doctrines of demons, by means of the hypocrisy of liars seared in their own conscience as with a branding iron, men who forbid marriage and advocate abstaining from foods which God has created to be gratefully shared in by those who believe and know the truth. For everything created by God is good, and nothing is to be rejected if it is received with gratitude; for it is sanctified by means of the word of God and prayer" (1Ti. 4:1-5).

Men of Depraved Mind and Deprived of the Truth

"If anyone advocates a different doctrine and does not agree with sound words, those of our Lord Jesus Christ, and with the doctrine conforming to godliness, he is conceited and understands nothing; but he has a morbid interest in controversial questions and disputes about words, out of which arise envy, strife, abusive language, evil suspicions, and constant friction between men of depraved mind and deprived of the truth, who suppose that godliness is a means of gain. But godliness actually is a means of great gain when accompanied by contentment. For we have brought nothing into the world, so we cannot take anything out of it either. If we have food and covering, with these we shall be content. But those who want to get rich fall into temptation and a snare and many foolish and harmful desires which plunge men into ruin and destruction. For the love of money is a root of all sorts of evil, and some by longing for it have wandered away from the faith and pierced themselves with many griefs" (1Ti. 6:3-10).

Accurately Handling the Word of Truth

"Remind them of these things, and solemnly charge them in the presence of God not to wrangle about words, which is useless and leads to the ruin of the hearers. Be diligent to present yourself approved to God as a workman who does not need to be ashamed, accurately handling the word of truth. But avoid worldly and empty chatter, for it will lead to further ungodliness, and their talk will spread like gangrene. Among them are Hymenaeus and Philetus, men who have gone astray from the truth saying that the resurrection has already taken place, and they upset the faith of some. Nevertheless, the firm foundation of God stands, having this seal, 'The Lord knows those who are His,' and, 'Everyone who names the name of the Lord is to abstain from wickedness'" (2Ti. 2:14-19).

Repentance Leading to the Knowledge of the Truth

"Now in a large house there are not only gold and silver vessels, but also vessels of wood and of earthenware, and some to honor and some to dishonor. Therefore, if anyone cleanses himself from these things, he will be a vessel for honor, sanctified, useful to the Master, prepared for every good work. Now flee from youthful lusts and pursue righteousness, faith, love and peace, with those who call on the Lord from a pure heart. But refuse foolish and ignorant speculations, knowing that they produce quarrels. The Lord's bond-servant must not be quarrelsome, but be kind to all, able to teach, patient when wronged, with gentleness correcting those who are in opposition, if perhaps God may grant them repentance leading to the knowledge of the truth, and they may come to their senses and escape from the snare of the devil, having been held captive by him to do his will" (2Ti. 2:20-26).

Never Able to Come to the Knowledge of the Truth

"But realize this, that in the last days difficult times will come. For men will be lovers of self, lovers of money, boastful, arrogant, revilers, disobedient to parents, ungrateful, unholy, unloving, irreconcilable, malicious gossips, without self-control, brutal, haters of good, treacherous, reckless, conceited, lovers of pleasure rather than lovers of God, holding to a form of godliness, although they have denied its power; Avoid such men as these. For among them are those who enter into households and captivate weak women weighed down with sins, led on by various impulses, always learning and never able to come to the knowledge of the truth. Just as Jannes and Jambres opposed Moses, so these men also oppose the truth, men of depraved mind, rejected in regard to the faith. But they will not make further progress; for their folly will be obvious to all, just as Jannes's and Jambres's folly was also. Now you followed my teaching, conduct, purpose, faith, patience, love, perseverance" (2Ti. 3:1-10).

Turn Away from the Truth and will Turn Aside to Myths

"I solemnly charge you in the presence of God and

of Christ Jesus, who is to judge the living and the dead, and by His appearing and His kingdom: preach the word; be ready in season and out of season; reprove, rebuke, exhort, with great patience and instruction. For the time will come when they will not endure sound doctrine; but wanting to have their ears tickled, they will accumulate for themselves teachers in accordance to their own desires, and will turn away their ears from the truth and will turn aside to myths. But you, be sober in all things, endure hardship, do the work of an evangelist, fulfill your ministry" (2Ti. 4:1-5).

Chosen of God and the Knowledge of the Truth

"Paul, a bond-servant of God and an apostle of Jesus Christ, for the faith of those chosen of God and the knowledge of the truth which is according to godliness, in the hope of eternal life, which God, who cannot lie, promised long ages ago, but at the proper time manifested, even His word, in the proclamation with which I was entrusted according to the commandment of God our Savior" (Tit. 1:1-3).

Men Who Turn Away from the Truth

"Who must be silenced because they are upsetting whole families, teaching things they should not teach for the sake of sordid gain. One of themselves, a prophet of their own, said, 'Cretans are always liars, evil beasts, lazy gluttons. This testimony is true. For this reason reprove them severely so that they may be sound in the faith, not paying attention to Jewish myths and commandments of men who turn away from the truth'" (Tit. 1:11-14).

Chapter Three

Sinning Willfully After Receiving the Truth

"For if we go on sinning willfully after receiving the knowledge of the truth, there no longer remains a sacrifice for sins, but a terrifying expectation of judgment and THE FURY OF A FIRE WHICH WILL CONSUME THE ADVERSARIES. Anyone who has set aside the Law of Moses dies without mercy on the testimony of two or three witnesses. How much severer punishment do you think he will deserve who has trampled under foot the Son of God, and has regarded as unclean the blood of the covenant by which he was sanctified, and has insulted the Spirit of grace? For we know Him who said, 'VENGEANCE IS MINE, I WILL REPAY.' And again, 'THE LORD WILL JUDGE HIS PEOPLE.' It is a terrifying thing to fall into the hands of the living God" (Heb. 10:26-31).

He Brought Us Forth by the Word of Truth

"Blessed is a man who perseveres under trial; for once he has been approved, he will receive the crown of life which the Lord has promised to those who love Him. Let no one say when he is tempted, 'I am being tempted by God'; for God cannot be tempted by evil, and He Himself does not tempt anyone. But each one is tempted when he is carried away and enticed by his own lust. Then when lust has conceived, it gives birth to sin; and when sin is accomplished, it brings forth death. Do not be deceived, my beloved brethren. Every good thing given and every perfect gift is from above, coming down from the Father of lights, with whom there is no variation or shifting shadow. In the exercise of His will He brought us forth by the word of truth, so that we would be a kind of first fruits among His creatures" (Jas. 1:12-18).

Chapter Three

Do Not Be Arrogant and So Lie Against the Truth

"Who among you is wise and understanding? Let him show by his good behavior his deeds in the gentleness of wisdom. But if you have bitter jealousy and selfish ambition in your heart, do not be arrogant and so lie against the truth. This wisdom is not that which comes down from above, but is earthly, natural, demonic. For where jealousy and selfish ambition exist, there is disorder and every evil thing. But the wisdom from above is first pure, then peaceable, gentle, reasonable, full of mercy and good fruits, unwavering, without hypocrisy. And the seed whose fruit is righteousness is sown in peace by those who make peace" (Jas. 3:13-18).

Strays from the Truth and One Turns Him Back

"My brethren, if any among you strays from the truth and one turns him back, let him know that he who turns a sinner from the error of his way will save his soul from death and will cover a multitude of sins" (Jas. 5:19-20).

In Obedience to the Truth Purified Your Souls

"Since you have in obedience to the truth purified your souls for a sincere love of the brethren, fervently love one another from the heart, for you have been born again not of seed which is perishable but imperishable, that is, through the living and enduring word of God. For, 'ALL FLESH IS LIKE GRASS, AND ALL ITS GLORY LIKE THE FLOWER OF GRASS. THE GRASS WITHERS, AND THE FLOWER FALLS OFF, BUT THE WORD OF THE LORD ENDURES FOREVER.' And this is the word which was preached to you" (1Pe. 1:22-25).

Chapter Three

Established in the Truth Which Is Present with You

"Therefore, I will always be ready to remind you of these things, even though you already know them, and have been established in the truth which is present with you. I consider it right, as long as I am in this earthly dwelling, to stir you up by way of reminder, knowing that the laying aside of my earthly dwelling is imminent, as also our Lord Jesus Christ has made clear to me. And I will also be diligent that at any time after my departure you will be able to call these things to mind" (2Pe. 1:12-15).

The Way of the Truth Will Be Maligned

"But false prophets also arose among the people, just as there will also be false teachers among you, who will secretly introduce destructive heresies, even denying the Master who bought them, bringing swift destruction upon themselves. Many will follow their sensuality, and because of them the way of the truth will be maligned; and in their greed they will exploit you with false words; their judgment from long ago is not idle, and their destruction is not asleep" (2Pe. 2:1-3).

We Lie and Do Not Practice the Truth

"This is the message we have heard from Him and announce to you, that God is Light, and in Him there is no darkness at all. If we say that we have fellowship with Him and yet walk in the darkness, we lie and do not practice the truth; but if we walk in the Light as He Himself is in the Light, we have fellowship with one another, and the blood of Jesus His Son cleanses us from all sin. If we say that we have no sin, we are deceiving ourselves and the truth is not in us. If we confess our sins,

He is faithful and righteous to forgive us our sins and to cleanse us from all unrighteousness. If we say that we have not sinned, we make Him a liar and His word is not in us" (1Jn. 1:5-10).

Is a Liar, and the Truth Is Not in Him

"By this we know that we have come to know Him, if we keep His commandments. The one who says, 'I have come to know Him,' and does not keep His commandments, is a liar, and the truth is not in him; but whoever keeps His word, in him the love of God has truly been perfected. By this we know that we are in Him: the one who says he abides in Him ought himself to walk in the same manner as He walked" (1Jn. 2:3-6).

Because You Do Not know the Truth

"Children, it is the last hour; and just as you heard that antichrist is coming, even now many antichrists have appeared; from this we know that it is the last hour. They went out from us, but they were not really of us; for if they had been of us, they would have remained with us; but they went out, so that it would be shown that they all are not of us. But you have an anointing from the Holy One, and you all know. I have not written to you because you do not know the truth, but because you do know it, and because no lie is of the truth. Who is the liar but the one who denies that Jesus is the Christ? This is the antichrist, the one who denies the Father and the Son. Whoever denies the Son does not have the Father; the one who confesses the Son has the Father also. As for you, let that abide in you which you heard from the beginning. If what you heard from the beginning abides in you, you also will abide in the Son and in the Father. This is the promise which He Himself made to us: eternal life" (1Jn. 2:18-25).

In Deed and Truth

"Do not be surprised, brethren, if the world hates you. We know that we have passed out of death into life, because we love the brethren. He who does not love abides in death. Everyone who hates his brother is a murderer; and you know that no murderer has eternal life abiding in him. We know love by this, that He laid down His life for us; and we ought to lay down our lives for the brethren. But whoever has the world's goods, and sees his brother in need and closes his heart against him, how does the love of God abide in him? Little children, let us not love with word or with tongue, but in deed and truth. We will know by this that we are of the truth, and will assure our heart before Him in whatever our heart condemns us; for God is greater than our heart and knows all things. Beloved, if our heart does not condemn us, we have confidence before God; and whatever we ask we receive from Him, because we keep His commandments and do the things that are pleasing in His sight" (1Jn. 3:13-22).

We Know the Spirit of Truth and the Spirit of Error

"Beloved, do not believe every spirit, but test the spirits to see whether they are from God, because many false prophets have gone out into the world. By this you know the Spirit of God: every spirit that confesses that Jesus Christ has come in the flesh is from God; and every spirit that does not confess Jesus is not from God; this is the spirit of the antichrist, of which you have heard that it is coming, and now it is already in the world. You are from God, little children, and have overcome them; because greater is He who is in you than he who is in the world.

They are from the world; therefore they speak as from the world, and the world listens to them. We are from God; he who knows God listens to us; he who is not from God does not listen to us. By this we know the spirit of truth and the spirit of error" (1Jn. 4:1-6).

The Spirit Is the Truth

"Who is the one who overcomes the world, but he who believes that Jesus is the Son of God? This is the One who came by water and blood, Jesus Christ; not with the water only, but with the water and with the blood. It is the Spirit who testifies, because the Spirit is the truth. For there are three that testify: the Spirit and the water and the blood; and the three are in agreement. If we receive the testimony of men, the testimony of God is greater; for the testimony of God is this, that He has testified concerning His Son. The one who believes in the Son of God has the testimony in himself; the one who does not believe God has made Him a liar, because he has not believed in the testimony that God has given concerning His Son. And the testimony is this, that God has given us eternal life, and this life is in His Son. He who has the Son has the life; he who does not have the Son of God does not have the life" (1Jn. 5:5-12).

Not Only I, but Also All Who Know the Truth

"The elder to the chosen lady and her children, whom I love in truth; and not only I, but also all who know the truth, for the sake of the truth which abides in us and will be with us forever: Grace, mercy and peace will be with us, from God the Father and from Jesus Christ, the Son of the Father, in truth and love" (2Jn. 1:1-3).

Chapter Three

Walking in Truth

"I was very glad to find some of your children walking in truth, just as we have received commandment to do from the Father. Now I ask you, lady, not as though I were writing to you a new commandment, but the one which we have had from the beginning, that we love one another. And this is love, that we walk according to His commandments. This is the commandment, just as you have heard from the beginning, that you should walk in it" (2Jn. 1:4-6).

My Children Walking in the Truth

"The elder to the beloved Gaius, whom I love in truth. Beloved, I pray that in all respects you may prosper and be in good health, just as your soul prospers. For I was very glad when brethren came and testified to your truth, that is, how you are walking in truth. I have no greater joy than this, to hear of my children walking in the truth" (3Jn. 1:1-4).

So that We May be Fellow Workers with the Truth

"Beloved, you are acting faithfully in whatever you accomplish for the brethren, and especially when they are strangers; and they have testified to your love before the church. You will do well to send them on their way in a manner worthy of God. For they went out for the sake of the Name, accepting nothing from the Gentiles. Therefore we ought to support such men, so that we may be fellow workers with the truth" (3Jn. 1:5-8).

From the Truth Itself

"Beloved, do not imitate what is evil, but what is good. The one who does good is of God; the one who does evil has not seen God. Demetrius has received a good testimony from everyone, and from the truth itself; and we add our testimony, and you know that our testimony is true" (3Jn. 1:11-12).

DAILY FAITH CONFESSIONS

(These are not direct quotations from the Bible but are paraphrased confessions based on scripture.)
SAY THEM OUT LOUD.

I am God's child (Jn. 1:12). I am royalty (1 Pet. 2:9). I am hidden with Christ in God (Col. 3:3). I am united with the Lord (1 Cor. 6:17). I am a friend of Christ (Jn. 15:15). I am raised up with Him, and seated with Him in heavenly places in Christ Jesus (Eph. 2:6). I was bought with a price (1 Cor. 6:19-20). I am blessed when I come in, and blessed shall I be when I go out (Deut. 28:6). I am a personal witness of Christ (Acts 1:8). I am a saint who prays in the Holy Spirit to keep myself in the love of God (Jude 1:20-21). I draw near with confidence to the throne of grace (Heb. 4:16). I have been adopted by the Father (Eph. 1:5). I am the salt and light of the earth (Mt. 5:13). I am the head and not the tail, and I am above, and not underneath (Deut. 28:13). I have authority to trample serpents and scorpions and over all the power of the enemy (Lk. 10:19). I am a member of the body of Christ (1 Cor. 12:27). God blessed me to be fruitful, and multiply, and replenish the earth, and subdue it: and have dominion (Gen. 1:28). I cannot be separated from God's love (Ro. 8:39). The good work God has begun in me will be perfected (Phil. 1:5). I can do all things through Christ who strengthens me (Phil. 4:13). No weapon that is formed against me will prosper (Is. 54:17). So then faith cometh by hearing, and hearing by the word of God (Ro. 10:17 KJV). Faith is my currency to operate in the kingdom of God (Ro. 14:23). I am God's workmanship created in Christ Jesus for good works, which God prepared beforehand (Eph. 2:10). I have been appointed to bear fruit, and that my fruit would remain (Jn. 15:16). I am being wise when I am winning souls for King Jesus (Pr. 11:30). My body is the temple of the Holy Spirit (1 Cor. 6:19). I have access to God through the Holy Spirit (Eph. 2:18). I have been justified (Ro. 5:1). Therefore there is now no condemnation for those who are in Christ Jesus (Ro. 8:1). Greater is He who is in me than he who is in the world (1 Jn. 4:4). I will do greater works than Jesus because He went to the Father (Jn. 14:12). As God was with Moses, He will be with me; God will not fail me or forsake me (Jos. 1:5). I see myself the way God see me. God sees me as a king (Gen, 17:6, Rev. 1:6) God sees me as royalty (1 Pet. 2:9). God sees me as the righteousness of God in Christ, bold as a lion (Ro. 3:22, Pr. 28:1). God sees me without spot or wrinkle because of the blood of Jesus (1 Pet. 1:19). I am having faith for big things because God owns everything and I'm His son (Ps. 24:1). No man will be able to stand before me all the days of my life (Jos. 1:5). My Father is glorified by this that I bear much fruit, and proves I'm a disciple (see Jn. 15:8). I think big and confess big things because God is big (Ps. 24:1). I will respect God for the big God that He is and my mouth will create whatever I want (Lk. 6:45). I no longer think of millions, my renewed mind thinks of billions because the wealth of the wicked is laid up for the righteous (Pr. 13:22). The sinner's job is to gather and collect for the one who is good in God's sight (Ecc. 2:26). Redemption is not complete without prosperity. Jesus hung on the cross so I can have the whole package, not just salvation (2 Cor. 8:9). I don't have to qualify, Jesus has qualified me. Jesus reversed the curse. The devil is a liar, and Jesus is the Messiah. Jesus is made unto to me wisdom, righteousness, sanctification, and redemption (1 Cor. 1:30). I submit to God, I resist the devil and he flees from me (Jas. 4:7). For God has not given me the spirit of fear; but of power, and of love, and of a sound mind (2 Tim. 1:7). The Holy Spirit will teach me all things (Jn. 14:26). The Holy Spirit will guide me into all truth (Jn.16:13). The Holy Spirit abides in me, and I don't need anyone to teach me, but the anointing teaches me all things (1 Jn. 2:27). I quench fiery darts from the wicked one with the shield of faith (Eph. 6:16). I stand firm against the schemes of the devil (Eph. 6:11). I already have the victory and Satan cannot back me up. I hold my position of consistent victory after victory (2 Cor. 2:14). I walk in love and live by faith (Gal. 5:6). I have been redeemed from the curse of the law, poverty, sickness, and spiritual death (Gal. 3:13; Deut. 28). I will bear so much fruit. I'm God's workmanship created beforehand for good works (Eph. 2:10). God's favor is on my life (Ps. 3:8). God blesses me and His favor surrounds me as with a shield (Ps. 5:12). The kingdom of God is within me (Lk. 17:21). I have a production plant inside of me that bears fruit to change the world (Gen. 1:28). God gives me power to get wealth to establish His covenant on earth (Deut. 8:18). I am blessed to be a blessing (Gen. 12:2). I have Satan on the run. I will make a mockery of him (Jas. 4:7). I'm spending forever with King Jesus (2 Cor. 5:8). Thank you Father. I love you!

PRAY FOR SALVATION

Say the following prayer out loud.

Heavenly Father, I am a sinner and I need a Savior. I confess Jesus Christ as the Lord of my life. I repent of all my sins. Father, I truly believe you raised Jesus from the dead. Father, give me spiritual hunger to spend time in Your Word day and night so my mind is renewed. I understand that by meditating and submitting to Your Word daily I will be transformed into the image of Jesus, day-by-day. Thank you, Father, for Your goodness, mercy, and grace. I pray in Jesus' name. Amen.

PRAYER FOR BAPTISM OF THE HOLY SPIRIT

Father, I am your child because Jesus is my Lord. Jesus said, "How much more shall your heavenly Father give the Holy Spirit to those who ask Him." I ask you now in the name of Jesus to fill me with the Holy Spirit. Thank you, Father, I received the baptism of the Holy Spirit by faith. I yield my vocal organs and expect to speak in tongues as the Holy Spirit gives me utterance in Jesus name. Father, I plan to pray in the Holy Spirit building myself up on my most holy faith, and keep myself in the love of God, as mentioned in Jude 20 and 21. In Jesus name I decree it. Amen.

ABOUT THE AUTHOR

Eugene Carvalho is the founder of Receiving by Faith. He is an administrator and Christian author of seventy books. God uses him in the offices of pastor, evangelist and prophet. He holds a bachelor's degree in biblical studies and a double minor in pastoral ministry and world missions. He also holds a master's degree in practical theology. Eugene prayed for a translator and God sent his wife Mercedes who has a six-year degree in Spanish from a university in Tampico, Mexico. They have participated in evangelism in the streets of Mexico for many years. They have also traveled to churches all over the United States and Mexico winning souls and preaching faith. Their current ministry website is: www.receivingbyfaith.org.

BOOKS BY EUGENE CARVALHO

To purchase other books by Eugene Carvalho visit receivingbyfaith.org or amazon.com.

Receiving by Faith
Faith for Every Day: 365 Daily Devotions
Faith Cometh by Hearing, and Hearing by the Word of God
Faith, Hope, and Love
Walk in Love and Live by Faith
Topical Christian Handbook and Scripture Guide
The Gospel Is the Power of God unto Salvation
Seed Time and Harvest Time
Your New Identity in Christ
The Cross and the Blood
The Holy Spirit
The Attributes of God
The Favor of God
The Glory of God
The Grace of God
The Power of God
The Promises of God
The Throne of God
The New Testament Church
Vengeance and Recompense
God's Angel's
Prayer and Fasting
God's Mighty Prophets
A Survey of Jesus Through the Epistles
The Names of Jesus
The Psalms of David

The Righteous Will Flourish like The Palm Tree
Old Testament Miracles
New Testament Miracles
Mountain Moving Confessions
Visions and Dreams
Blessed Beyond Measure
Christ Heals: What the Bible Has to Say
My Peace I Give to You
Balancing Grace and Truth
Praise and Worship Changes Everything
Understanding the Importance of Authority
If You Are Willing and Obedient
Have Life More Abundantly
Sing Unto the Lord a New Song
The Power of the Tongue
The Supernatural: What the Bible Has to Say
The Truth Will Make You Free
Joy in the Holy Ghost
Praise Is Powerful: What the Bible Has to Say
Stewardship Regarding Our Finances
Love, Joy, and Peace Are Fruit of the Holy Ghost
Oh, Give Thanks to the Lord for He Is Good
The Kingdom of Heaven is at Hand
Acquiring Wisdom Is Vital
Grace and Mercy: What the Bible Has to Say
God Is Faithful: What the Bible Has to Say
God Is Love: What the Bible Has to Say
The God of Hope: What the Bible Has to Say
Pearls of Wisdom and Gems of Knowledge
Regarding Christianity
Victory is Mine, Joy is Mine, Peace Is Mine: I Told
Satan to Get Thee Behind

The Master's Gems
For the Kingdom of God Is Righteousness, Peace and Joy in the Holy Ghost
Encountering Proverbs, Ecclesiastes, and Song of Solomon Through a Topical Survey
Prayer Is Powerful: What the Bible Has to Say
My People Are Destroyed By Lack of Knowledge
Striving Toward Perfection
God Deserves Pure Worship
The Lord Requires Integrity: The Major Element of Leadership
A Topical Look at the Book of Deuteronomy
A Topical Look at the Book of Psalms
A Topical Look at the Book of Proverbs
A Topical Look at the Book of Isaiah
A Topical Look at the Book of John
A Topical Look at the Book of Hebrews
A Topical Look at the Book of Revelation

BOOKS BY EUGENE IN SPANISH

Las Promesas de Dios
Los Salmos de David
Lo Sobrenatural: Lo que la Bíblia Tiene que Decir
Una Mirada Topica Del Libro De Los Salmos
Dios es Amor: Lo que la Biblia Tiene que Decir
La Adquisición de la Sabiduría es Vital: Lo que la
Biblia Tiene que Decir

NOTES

NOTES

NOTES

www.ingramcontent.com/pod-product-compliance
Lightning Source LLC
Chambersburg PA
CBHW061716250726
48657CB00002B/629